the face of home

the face of home

a new way to look at the outside of your house

Jeremiah Eck, FAIA

The Taunton Press

The Taunton Press
Inspiration for hands-on living®

The Taunton Press, Inc., 63 South Main Street, PO Box 5506, Newtown, CT
06470-5506
e-mail: tp@taunton.com

Editors: Peter Chapman, Scott Gibson
Jacket/Cover design: Alexander Isley, Inc.
Interior design and layout: Jeannet Leendertse
Illustrator: Christine Erikson

THE AMERICAN INSTITUTE
OF ARCHITECTS

The American Institute of Architects, founded in 1857, is a professional
society of architects with over 70,000 members in the United States and
abroad. Through its national, regional, state, and local components, the AIA
works to achieve more humane built environments and higher standards
of professionalism for architects through education, government advocacy,
community redevelopment, and public outreach activities. AIA's website is
located at aia.org.

AIA, The American Institute of Architects, and the AIA logo are registered
trademarks and service marks of The American Institute of Architects.

This book is published under the joint imprint of The American Institute of
Architects and The Taunton Press, Inc.

Library of Congress Cataloging-in-Publication Data

Eck, Jeremiah.
  The face of home : a new way to look at the outside of your house / Jeremiah
Eck.
     p. cm.
  ISBN-13: 978-1-56158-771-1
  ISBN-10: 1-56158-771-0
  1. Architecture--United States--Details. 2. Architecture, Domestic--United
States. 3. Landscape architecture--United States. I. Title.
  NA2840.E23 2006
  728'.37--dc22
                                      2005029666

Printed in the United States of America
10 9 8 7 6 5 4 3 2 1

To my father, who showed me through his example that curiosity
and courage are a large part of intelligence

acknowledgments

Writing a book is like building a house. Books and houses are
both put together by so many people that it's often hard to single
out any individual who made it all possible. Nevertheless, some
stand out.

First, the staff at The Taunton Press, who didn't believe me when
I said I'd never write another book after *The Distinctive Home*
in 2003. Everyone at Taunton, from publisher Jim Childs and
editor-in-chief Maria Taylor on down, was wonderful to work
with. Most of all, thanks to Peter Chapman. Had he not agreed
to be my editor, I would have stuck to my declaration. Any
meaningful human endeavor, like writing a book, requires great
attention to detail. I happen to believe it also requires a certain
sense of humor since absolute perfection is never possible.
Peter has both qualities in spades. Thanks, too, to Scott Gibson,
who polished off my inadequate efforts at the Queen's English
and provided the subtle support that kept me focused, and to
my partners Paul MacNeely and Steve Mielke who, once again,
tolerated the time taken away from the office for such a task.

Finally, thanks to all those who contributed to this book: to the
homeowners who first dreamed of these houses; the architects
who designed them; and the contractors who built them. Each
house is proof of their collective genius and passion. My words
can never fully describe them.

contents

introduction

Every night on my way home from work, I drive past a brand-new home that presents an absolutely blank wall to the road. There's not a window or door or any other distinguishing feature in sight, just a sea of shining vinyl siding. Barely 200 yards up the same road, there's another house with a two-story entry foyer that a fully grown giraffe could easily walk through. Drive a bit farther and you'll come to a house that greets visitors with a three-bay garage like an open mouth.

Let's face it. There are a lot of ugly houses out there. Many of them are massively overscaled, designed more to impress than to inspire, with towering facades and schizophrenic rooflines. Why is it that Americans build so many ugly houses each year? I've asked myself that question for a long time, not just as an architect who designs houses for a living but also as a person who cares about the world around him. To my mind, an ugly house pollutes our visual environment just as much as hazardous waste pollutes our land. I'm convinced that much of the sprawl problem we denounce so often could be solved, in part, by simply building more beautiful homes. Such houses would truly belong to the sites they sit on and be infinitely more pleasing to look at and live in.

In my first book, *The Distinctive Home: A Vision of Timeless Design*, I argued that a truly distinctive home is the result of a subtle balance between the site, the floor plan, the exterior, and the architectural detailing, and that all four should reinforce each other. Exteriors, what I call the "faces" of home, are part of that balance, but the process of producing a distinctive exterior is not always understood or described adequately by many of the people who build, buy, and even design most houses today. In *The Face of Home*, we'll take a detailed look at five simple hallmarks of good design for house exteriors.

When most people describe the exterior of a house, they give it a label or identify it by a particular style. They might say, for example, that they live in the colonial down the street, or that they're going to buy a contemporary. But in truth what they are referring to is a combination of physical characteristics, such as rooflines, windows, or porches, and the emotional impact all of these things make collectively—whether the exterior seems inviting, austere, or even grand. This book will examine these physical and emotional characteristics in detail and give you a way of understanding house exteriors that goes well beyond simple labels.

Labels have their place, but they're not the only way and certainly not the best way of describing a house. In designing houses, we'd be better off allowing the face of home to evolve on its own (we can always give it a label later). If your approach to the exterior of your house is thoughtful and considers the hallmarks I explain in this book, it won't matter whether people describe it as traditional, contemporary, or something else entirely. It won't matter because it will be just right.

It's not enough to examine the physical and emotional characteristics of a house exterior in isolation. They should be weighed in the context of the whole house. An exterior elevation is not the product of some independent process that's applied after the fact, but the result of a back-and-forth examination of inside and outside. The notion that elevations are separate, almost decorative, elements is one that pervades the American market. Refuting that idea by showing that they are an integral part of the whole design process is one of the major reasons for writing this book. I hope you will find the hallmarks and the house examples that illustrate them both useful and inspiring. Although most houses built today are just plain ugly, we can do better. We've done it before and we can do it again.

reading
the face of home

Picture your favorite house. Whether it's Fallingwater by Frank Lloyd Wright, Greene and Greene's Gamble House, or a nameless cottage by the shore, you probably have in mind a single image of the exterior. Similarly, when a real estate agent lists a house, the defining photo is invariably of the outside. Even a child's first drawing of a house typically shows a simple exterior with a few windows, a door, and a chimney. Of all the ways we can describe a house, it's the outside we relate to first, but the exterior is also the most misunderstood element of a house. Is it there simply to give the house "curb appeal" or is there a more significant meaning behind the "face of home"?

why the "face of home"?

On the simplest level, "face" just refers to the outward appearance, the way the house looks on the outside. But on a deeper level, a house exterior can be just as expressive as the human face, revealing character, creating a first impression, and telling us something about the inner workings and organization of the building (see the photos below left). The face is typically a person's most distinctive characteristic, the one we notice first. House exteriors—what I'm calling their faces—are also the first things we notice (see the photos on the facing page).

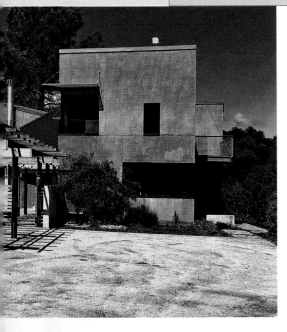

Whether intentionally or not, houses often have exterior sides that look like faces.

The palette of house parts—roofs, windows, and doors—can look like hats, eyes, and noses.

All human faces have roughly the same proportions. The eyes, nose, mouth, and ears are centered on the head, and the relative distance from one feature to another is about the same. In other words, the composition or proportions of all human faces are generally consistent. Yet, amazingly, no two faces look exactly alike. Within the almost universal proportions of the human face lies an almost infinite variety. A slight change in the size of the lips or the nose can make one person look very different from another. A slight change of expression can tell you something about how they feel.

Similarly, houses have a common palette of parts and materials, such as roofs, windows, doors, and siding, and the variations are endless. You can carry the face metaphor further by saying windows are like eyes, doors can look like noses, and, in some of the worst of today's examples, the garage looks like a gaping mouth from the street. And, as with faces, minor adjustments to the parts or materials of a house exterior can make a big difference in how it looks or feels. Of course, the metaphor can only be carried so far since houses, unlike people, really have more than one face. Nonetheless, the basic premise of this book, that the face of home is important to our fundamental understanding of house and that its varieties can be elegant and almost infinite, holds true.

In a well-designed house, the inside and the outside are closely related to each other. You should be able to tell what's going on inside the house by looking at the outside.

A new way of looking at the face of home

To start thinking about a new way of looking at house exteriors, let's take an up-close look at one of the houses that our firm designed in Lincoln, Massachusetts, just west of Boston (see the photo below). I'll talk about this house in more detail later in the book (see pp. 60–69), but, for now, let's just look at the entry face. What's your first impression when you look at this side? Maybe you find yourself searching for a label for this house: Is it traditional or contemporary? Does this style have a name? These are the usual questions we might ask about a house we're seeing for the first time, but they don't get us very far. At best, all we will get is a label that doesn't mean very much. A better approach is to look closely at the house and begin to pull it apart visually, in a way to deconstruct it. The most prominent features on this side of the house are the two gables that flank the entry. Even though the two gables are of different sizes, the arrangement is pleasing because they appear to be in balance. But why are they asymmetrical, with one larger gable jutting out past the other? If you could look inside, you'd see that the smaller gable houses a bathroom and the larger a bedroom. The relative sizes are appropriate to their use.

The gables are but one component on the exterior. Other features stand out, too. Take a look at the siding treatment. There are two horizontal siding materials of two different colors; one is narrow clapboard, the other wide. Why the different treatment? One helps define the upper floor of the house, while the other is more connected to the lower floor. The portion of narrow white clapboard under the overhang just to the left of the glass entry doors ties into the gable above, making it seem bigger, and it also helps bring it in balance with the larger gable to the right. The white color ties into the color of the bracket, the trim, and the entry door, making the whole entry more pleasing than it would have been, say, if there had been all the same clapboard of the same color.

Looking next at the windows, you'll notice that there are a number of different styles and sizes. Yet even with all this variety, the exterior is still in balance. This "face of home" looks the way it does not only because of the need to make a pleasing exterior but also to fulfill practical requirements. The two should never be separate and must always be weighed together. To apply an exterior look without taking into account what goes on inside is just as wrong as designing an interior function and then not caring about what it looks like outside. The rest of this book is dedicated to showing how that balance is achieved and how houses with successful exteriors are almost always characterized by the same hallmarks of good design. As a point of departure, though, let's start with the language of houses we already know, the conventional architectural labels we use to describe what houses look like.

No part of a house exterior should be arbitrary. All parts should be in balance and tell you a story about the whole house, inside and out.

Roof brackets lend visual support to the wide overhang and provide another detail in the complexion of this face.

Slot windows in the gable are a nice visual contrast to the larger exterior windows, and they provide light to the high ceiling within.

Glass doors, transoms, and three windows above the low roof at the second floor all signal main entry and flood the entry hall with light.

Two clay chimney pots act as exclamation points on the stone chimney.

Three 2-over-1 windows at the mudroom are ganged together to form a bay that balances the two-story gable.

The water table creates a more pleasing transition between the ground and body of the house.

A change in color at the entry wall helps tie the entry to the gable above, making that gable seem larger and balancing it with the gable to the right.

A change in siding material and color helps differentiate the first floor from the second floor and gives the house a more human scale.

Large 2-over-1 windows balance the smaller windows on the second floor and provide corner views for the first-floor office inside.

the old way of reading

If we want to talk about the face of home, we need to have a common frame of reference or an associated language that goes with it. In the past, a variety of house labels were devised. They are typically descriptive terms that place a house in a particular time or place or associate it with a particular shape, material, or even architect. By using a label to describe a house, we conjure up its attributes and get some hints on how we are to "read" or look at the exterior. This is fine as far as it goes, but the trouble is that labels are not always consistent, nor are they complete or totally accurate.

A Dutch-inspired gambrel roof is not only elegant but also reflects a fundamental need to gain more usable room on the second floor.

Georgian and Federal-style houses were symmetrical and larger than their predecessors because of increasing American wealth.

The mansard roof is actually a four-sided gambrel roof and creates even more headroom on the second floor.

Labels from national origins or historical periods

If I describe the exterior of a house as Dutch colonial or Georgian, certain images will come to mind. Dutch colonial will probably mean a somewhat boxy, one-and-a-half-story house with a gambrel roof and a flared edge or eave. A Georgian—or the later, more restrained Federal—will conjure up images of a balanced, essentially symmetrical exterior reinforced by a chimney at each end and some ornate detailing, particularly at windows and doors. Even though these are familiar images, the labels for these houses don't really explain why these faces of the past look the way they do.

Borrowing from earlier building traditions, the Dutch settlers used the gambrel roof to gain more room on the cramped second floor; the flared eaves shed rainwater and snow. The exterior was actually the result of specific size and environmental concerns as well as what was going on inside. It's true that Georgian and Federal houses look well balanced, but more important is that the houses had larger rooms and higher ceilings because an expanding merchant class had money to spend on better houses.

More than any other house type, the Cape personifies humble early American house origins.

Labels from locations, shapes, or materials

Sometimes a region can provide the name for a house style. The Cape from Cape Cod elicits a strong visual image of a low slung, single-story house with a simple roof, a dominant center chimney, and spartan detailing. But the term by itself tells us nothing of the reasoning behind the exterior. In the 18th century, life in the Northeast centered around the chimney, both socially and functionally (and before the days of building codes, the chimney provided some structural support). Its hunkered-down look says just that. It's interesting to compare the center-chimney colonials and Capes from the Northeast with the center-hall counterparts of the South during the same period where social conditions and the environment were quite different and required a much more open plan.

Houses have been given labels that refer to their physical qualities, such as their shapes or the materials they're made from: for example, the saltbox, split-level ranch, and bungalow. In a way, these exterior descriptions are the most honest labels because they offer an explanation of what the house looks like or what it's made of. A New England saltbox of the 18th century was given its name because its exterior shape was similar to a saltbox. Even in this case, the distinctive north-facing roof, similar to the lid of a saltbox, was also there to block harsh winter winds and give just a bit more room on the upper floor. Even the 20th century's ubiquitous split-level ranch clearly defines what you are looking at: a long, usually, low house divided in half levels. The descriptive label was clear and straightforward and actually begins to get at my idea behind this book—that exteriors are the result of a design process that takes into account the site, plan, and other principles I will describe later. Exteriors are more than just a name.

Seeking the *why* behind the *what*

Although these house labels give us an idea of where the building belongs in our historical frame of reference, they tend to focus on the "what" rather than the "why." In a sense, they become an impediment to understanding the design characteristics because they don't help us ask the right questions. There is another way of looking at houses, one that puts artificial labels aside and helps us to understand the authentic face of home and the principles that lie behind it.

The distinguishing characteristics of most bungalows are steep main roofs with large overhangs and continuous, low-sloped porch roofs.

Architects sometimes spawn their own labels, such as this Frank Lloyd Wrightean example.

The so-called saltbox was given its name because of the long sloping north-facing roof that protected the inhabitants from the harsh winter.

looking beyond labels: a new way to read exteriors

In many of the houses being built today, it's almost as though the exteriors have been pasted on like veneer, with no apparent regard for what's going on inside the house. There's no connection between the exterior and either the site or the interior floor plan. These houses look confused because they are confused. Towering two-story entry foyers and manic rooflines (see the photo below) leave me with an uneasy, out-of-control feeling. Exterior detailing like brick veneer or aluminum gutters that double as exterior trim is unconvincing and ungainly. These houses are often given labels that don't explain very much: Calling a big, awkward house a "modern colonial" or a "French country chateau" doesn't help us understand much about it. Worse, those labels can actually obscure what the house exteriors are really about.

What we need is a new way of looking at our houses, one based on basic design principles that collectively serve as a reference in assessing house exteriors. These are the hallmarks of good design, characteristics that all well-designed houses share no matter the particular architectural style or materials used to build them. If we begin to look at houses in a fresh way, we won't need misleading or simplistic labels. We'll gain a deeper understanding of how a successful exterior is assembled and how inside and outside can relate to each other, to the site, and to the plan.

Large, oversized entries that are rarely used are all too often characteristic of many houses built today.

Other houses are sited in ways that make the relation to the land awkward and their yards barely usable.

first impressions: site and house are one

Where do you start if you're trying to understand how a "face" gets put together? First, you need to take a step back and observe its overall shape and scale and how it relates to its site. Instead of just a two-dimensional "face," you're looking at a three-dimensional "head." One of the techniques that many painters use to judge the quality of a painting is to step back once in a while and squint at it. This may sound odd because squinting is not really about seeing something clearly. But the technique is useful because it allows you to see only the major elements of the painting without getting stuck on the details. If the overall composition of the painting doesn't work from a distance, no amount of detail will ever save it.

The same is true of houses. They can look different from a distance than they do up close. My initial read always starts by considering the house in a very general way from a distance, much as a visitor might and something like squinting at a painting. After all, this is how we all see a house at first. It's just like seeing someone on the street. From a distance, you might notice only his overall shape, but as you move closer the details of body, face, and hair become more distinct. Much like a person's face, an exterior or face of a house from a distance is about big statements. Looking at the Virginia house (see the photos at left and below), what you notice first is the way the house seems to hug the old road and how the roof shapes,

From a distance and close up, a good face of home should feel comfortable with its surroundings and be made of materials that blend with the site.

Whether a house is in a rural setting or on a suburban lot, it should feel as if it belongs to the land.

One of the reasons many houses built today seem out of place is that they have no connection to their sites. It's almost as if they could be located anywhere. If identical houses are built in, say, the Arizona desert and a Maine forest, how can the design be responding well to both sites? Just as important is where the house is placed on the property, another element of siting. I once lived down the street from a large house under construction. As I watched it being built, with its oversized entry and large columns, I noticed there was actually no way to get from the sidewalk to the front door (see the photo below). You could only get into the house from the garage. That's hardly a well-sited house. Careful siting won't save an inherently poor design, but even a fundamentally good house design gets off on the wrong foot if siting has been mishandled.

It's not always easy to point to a specific feature of a well-sited house—the way it nestles into the side of a hill, for instance, or how it faces a distant view—because in truth the more a house blends with the landscape the more invisible its siting becomes. It will be hard to see the house and land separately. That's the point.

especially the front porch with its overhang, reinforce that feeling. The colors of the chimney, the reddish-brown metal roof, and even the white siding blend with the surrounding landscape. It's only when you move closer that its other details began to take shape. As with the eyes, nose, or lines on a face, you begin to see more detail—here, the logs, the individual stones of the chimney, and the clapboard and board-and-batten siding.

Another way of saying this is that house and site are one. It's the first hallmark of a good face of home. You can't look at the face in isolation; it has to be considered in the context of its location. Just how the house is positioned on the land, what architects call "siting," has an obvious impact on how it looks. To me, no exterior can be truly distinctive or beautiful unless the house has been well sited, meaning that it seems to belong to the landscape rather than posing as an uncomfortable guest. This should be true whether the house is by itself along the ocean, on a suburban lot (see the photos at left), or in a dense urban neighborhood (see the photo above).

In spite of its gigantic entry porches and doors, this recently built house doesn't offer a way to get from the sidewalk to the front door.

full face: mass and scale are balanced

We've looked at the house from a distance and thought about the way it's sited, whether in an open field or a crowded urban neighborhood. Now we begin to near the house, seeing it not quite face-to-face but close enough to get the big picture— its shape and form. That leads to the second hallmark of any good face of home: a well-designed exterior should have balanced massing and scale.

The perception of size can be manipulated by changing mass and scale. Even houses with the same square footage (see the photos below and on the facing page) can appear to be of different size.

Massing and *scale* are architectural terms that generally have to do with the house in three dimensions: height, length, and width. Although they are related ideas, they aren't the same. Mass is volume or bulk; scale concerns the relative size of house elements, particularly as they relate to a person. Two houses could have exactly the same square footage, and even equal volumes, but look completely different in size because their mass and scale are different (see the photos at left and below). These are characteristics you always notice at some distance. The correct use of scale and massing can make a large house feel small and, surprisingly, make a small house feel large.

Breaking down the mass of this house into a number of more easily comprehended parts helps it achieve an intimate scale.

It would certainly make designing houses easier if there were some ironclad rule we could use to get the mass and scale right, a simple formula that unerringly produced the right answer. But there isn't one. Evaluating these two characteristics is more subjective. It requires looking at the sum of the parts, the total picture, and asking whether the house seems in balance. When I look at a house close up for the first time, I ask whether it feels right in the third dimension. In other words, does it have a pleasing mass—not too big, not too heavy— and does the scale feel right, meaning that I'd feel comfortable standing next to it. Even large houses that at first seem only massive can have the right scale when their various parts relate easily and naturally to each other (see the photo above).

Houses with a large mass don't have to be ugly. Compare the way similar elements such as roofs, windows, and entries are used in these two examples, one balanced, the other awkward.

The massing and scale of many houses built today just seem plain wrong (see the photo at left). Massing tends to be too boxy or clunky, and scale seems out of proportion to the people who use the house. Think of a house with an absurdly high entryway and enormous exterior columns. It looks completely out of proportion to anyone who might live there. For the most part, a house with good scale—the right size for its surrounding and occupants—will also have good massing, one that feels appropriate in bulk and weight.

Two well-defined second-floor bedroom bays with multiple overhangs give this house a more balanced and pleasing mass.

Designing porches that people can really use is often a good way of achieving better massing and scale at the same time.

Roofs are an important characteristic of mass and scale and can help a house fit the site.

There are many elements that can give a house an appropriate scale and mass from a distance. A large house can be broken down into a number of smaller masses or wings. You might reduce the mass by cantilevering the second floor over the first floor or by adding dormers, towers, balconies, bays, and chimneys (see the photo at left). All those features can help bring a house into balance when it would seem too chunky or massive by itself.

Roof shape is another important component. Using a high-pitched roof over the second floor and a lower-pitched roof over a portion of the first floor helps reduce mass. That's one reason why porch roofs are often so appealing (see the photo below left). There are many types of roofs—gable, hip, shed, gambrel, flat, and so on—and while none is inherently better than the others, a roof should help the house connect with its site. For instance, if a house is perched atop a gently sloping hill, an umbrella-like shape or a low-sloped shed might be better than a flat roof because it looks something like the summit of the hill (see the photo below). In a crowded neighborhood of older homes with some historical significance, a steep roof with multiple dormers might look best because it fits in with what's around it even if other parts of the house are more contemporary. In a way, roofs are like hats. It's hard to look beyond one that sits awkwardly on its owner's head.

behind the face: the plan is a guide

A common mistake people make is to look at a house and see the exterior as something independent of the floor plan. Homeowners and even designers often see the inside and outside as different realms, as if you could design the outside and inside of the house separately. Exactly the opposite is true, and this is one of the reasons why so many houses built today seem to have arbitrary and haphazard exteriors. The jumble of shapes doesn't seem to tell us anything about what's going on inside. In a well-designed house, the plan shows itself on the exterior; what we see as we look at the house from the outside is a kind of guide to its interior.

In a well-designed house, the outside suggests what's going on inside. Here, a large window dominating one end of this Maine cottage tells you where to find an important room inside.

These roof dormers are not arbitrary. They are balanced on the exterior and tell you something about the quality of the bedroom space inside.

One way to think of it is to imagine the exterior elevation as the floor plan figuratively turned on its side. The two should make sense together. A room with a high ceiling should feel the same way on the exterior. How? A large room would likely have large windows and therefore should read more "open" on the exterior than, say, a small room with small windows (see the photos on the facing page). Protruding bays or roofs with dormers also have something to say about a house interior. If there's a dormer on a roof, it may be telling you there's a bedroom, study, or home office inside, a special space that justified the added trouble of raising the roof for more light, air, and headroom (see the photos on this page). Creating a floor plan that reads on the exterior may seem subtle, but what it means is that floor plan and exterior will be integrated. The combined effect will show a certain logic.

face to face: parts are in harmony

As you move closer to a house, you begin to focus less on the big picture and more on the details. For the first time, you see the house up close, face-to-face. Massing and scale are still important, but now the details become more obvious. We know that every house is going to have walls, windows, doors, and color, but how do all these pieces hang together in a pleasing way? The answer is that all of the components must harmonize with one another, whether the house is large or small, symmetrical or asymmetrical, there are many elements to consider in the compositional puzzle: roof overhangs, the size and placement of windows and doors, the texture of the siding, a detail on the chimney, even color. All are elements of a larger puzzle that must make sense visually when they are brought together to form a whole.

A simple continuous pergola helps tie the various structures of this house together, demonstrating that even asymmetrical houses can look harmonious.

One clue that house parts are not working with each other is when you begin making mental alterations to the exterior. The house might seem to be missing a porch roof over the front door, a bay at the kitchen window, or a larger roof overhang. If these kinds of questions begin to nag at us, it suggests the house needs some adjustments at this level of observation and that the exterior isn't fully resolved.

Material focus

Something you're likely to notice right off about someone you meet on the street is his clothing and the fabric it's made from. The same is true of a house. Consider for a minute the materials you could use to finish the exterior of a house. Wood is the most common in this country, but brick, stone, block, stucco, steel, even rammed earth are other options. Choosing one over another produces a number of effects, and different materials can also be combined on the same house.

It doesn't matter what material you use: Wood, stone, even steel, all can help harmonize the face of a house.

A change from clapboards on the first floor to shingles on the second gives this house a more interesting look than a single material would have produced.

Take just two common wall materials—wood shingles and clapboards. Regularly spaced clapboards create a series of horizontal lines across a building exterior, while wood shingles have a less uniform, more textured quality. Our office sometimes combines the two on a single wall, shingles below and clapboards above or vice versa (see the photo at left). This approach sets up a harmony between the two materials much like two singers might make. The resulting sound— or, in this case, look—is often more appealing than one material alone. Materials have to harmonize with where and how they are used. Unstained wood shingles look just fine on a seashore house but not great in a more urban setting. Finely detailed brick walls look great in the city but hopelessly out of place in the woods.

A simple shaped house often looks best with a simple roof.

Windows, even doors, can be considered the "eyes" of a house since they look at the world beyond and even tell us something important about what lies within.

The choice of roofing material can have a similar effect. As is the case with walls, there are a limited number of choices. Slate, metal, wood, asphalt/fiberglass, and rubber are the most common. A metal roof is generally of a uniform color without much texture; it feels right on smaller, simpler houses such as cottages or farmhouses (see the photo above). A wood shingle roof has a lot of texture and works well when there is more elaborate wood detailing on the rest of the house (the so-called Shingle Style houses of the 19th century are a great example of this phenomenon).

Windows: the eyes of a house

The size and arrangement of windows (and doors) is probably the number-one factor in determining the face of home. If the roof is a kind of hat for the house, then the windows are its eyes. Of course, siting and floor plan considerations help to determine the positioning, size, and to some extent the type of windows and doors that are used. But these elements also have an independent rhythm, one that has to do with creating parts in harmony.

Windows don't always have to be perfectly aligned one over the other to create an interesting effect. This small historical house is a good example.

This southern colonial just wouldn't look right if the parts were not symmetrical.

There are a few simple rules about the placement of windows and doors. They should not only take advantage of views, sunlight, and ventilation but also correspond to the location and relative importance of rooms in the plan. In other words, they should be tied to the site and plan as we described in hallmarks one and three. Their size and placement should also form a balanced composition within the overall massing and scale of the house as we discussed in hallmark two. And they should blend easily with siding, trim, and the texture of exterior materials.

The placement of windows and doors isn't easy. You might assume that once you've got the plan right and the walls in the right places then the windows will follow, but that's not the case. Windows come in many different sizes, and they can be placed in a number of ways even when taking the plan into consideration. The goal should be to achieve a balance between all the window and door sizes on the exterior and the placement of those windows and doors on the walls. To get an idea of what I mean by this balance, start with a perfectly symmetrical façade, like a typical colonial that has an obvious balance of windows and doors, and begin changing their size and placement. You'll probably see right away why the original was better and why such a strong order was and remains so popular (see the photo above right).

Color: the forgotten tool

When most people think about the color of a house, they think about paint colors. While it's true that you can buy a couple of gallons of paint and dramatically change the color of the outside of your house, color is more than just applied paint; it's also integral to all the materials of the house, from the foundation to the roof. Whether the color is natural or applied, think of exteriors as a palette of colors that should be coordinated—just as we try to coordinate colors in our clothes.

The natural color of the body and complementary trim of this house are important ingredients in making its faces compatible with its surroundings.

Color can emphasize different parts of a building, in this case giving individual units of a large housing project their own identities.

In this house, a unifying effect is created by staining the body and trim of the house the same color.

When trim color is the same as the siding, it helps to unify a design (see the top left photo on the facing page). When it's different—painted trim paired with a natural siding, for example—it can help to define different siding choices, like makeup on a face. A brightly colored stucco house in the city, for instance, sends an expressive message, while a wood house in the country left to weather naturally likely blends in more with the surrounding environment.

The color of the roof often represents the first color choice for any house and so it helps to establish a color palette. Green and red are the two most dramatic colors available in asphalt/fiberglass shingles, but they can sometimes look too dramatic. On the other hand, a more subdued colored roof such as gray or black works well with almost any color used elsewhere on the exterior.

More than one face

One thing to remember as you consider how materials, colors, and house features get along with each other is that a house has more than one face (see the photos below). Most houses actually have four faces possibly more, and not all elevations have to be the same because each side of the house faces a different part of the site and fronts a different part of the floor plan. At the same time, each face should tie into adjacent walls. After all, every house is a three-dimensional object, usually seen from more than one side at once. As you approach a house, you're often seeing more than one face simultaneously. This is why many new houses are so glaringly unsuccessful. It's not uncommon to see a house with a grand, brick-faced exterior on the side of the house facing the street, while the vinyl-clad sidewalls are virtually devoid of windows and any other detailing. Unless each side of the house can contribute to the whole, the exterior just won't work.

No house has only one face. It's important that each face ties into adjacent walls so that the house feels like a whole.

complexion: details spring from the whole

No book about the face of home would be complete without a discussion of exterior details. Sharply focused details are the fine points of any house, something that ultimately gives it character. Exterior details should flow naturally from the other choices that have already been made. For instance, if a porch is an important feature of the exterior, then it should have distinctive details, such as delicate roof edges or an interesting siding material that helps it stand out from the rest of the house.

Texture makes an impact

I mentioned siding as an exterior material earlier, but there's another, more detailed aspect to it—its inherent texture or patterning. Wood siding can generally be bought with a smooth or rough side, while block, brick, and stone come in different dimensions and textures. Each choice brings with it a certain pattern that can add some additional life to the quality of an exterior—a vertical or horizontal emphasis, for instance, or a different kind of shadow pattern (see the photos at left and below).

The inherent textures of different building materials make an important contribution to the overall character of a house.

In this unusual detail, battens are carried beyond the boards at the base of the house to create a more interesting transition between house and ground.

Much like clothing accessories, trim can help differentiate and emphasize separate siding materials.

Trim also has a role to play. For instance, a wide horizontal trim board at the midpoint of an exterior wall might be useful in separating shingles and clapboards on the first and second floors (see the photo above). Or you might apply thin vertical boards or battens over flat boards to create a rhythm of vertical shadow lines (see the photo above right). The texture or patterning that is achieved by the choice of material or the way it is applied can produce a touch of elegance or a rustic quality, playfully highlight a particular pattern, or establish a rigid order. Whatever the detail, it should spring naturally from earlier decisions—it's not a time to try something completely new that doesn't relate to the larger house components that have already been established.

Edges are the lines between the parts

The edges of a house—the small areas between the ground and the wall above it and between the wall and the roof—are details that are often overlooked, but for me they are among the most important features of a house exterior. An elegant detail used here can unify the exterior of a house in a unique way. This is where the body and the roof of the house start and stop, where the house meets the ground and the sky. These two details are generally known as the *water table* and the roof *rake* and *eave*. Simply running the wall material straight to the ground without some terminating detail, or having no trim between the roof and walls, is seldom the right choice. It's like having a shirt without cuffs or collar. Borders here might be made from the same siding material as the rest of the house— clapboards, say, that are tightly spaced—or a solid piece of wood painted another color.

Accessories should relate to the whole

I think of features like chimneys, brackets, columns, rails, and trellises as exclamation points on a house, almost like accessories you might wear.

Nothing transmits a sense of warmth and comfort like a chimney; nothing but a chimney says there's a hearth on the interior. More than anything else, the power of a chimney comes from the materials it's made from. Stone makes sense if there's a lot of stone in the area or if the rest of the house is stone; stucco works fine if the rest of the house is stucco or if the chimney is not too large or overly complicated. Brick allows a number of interesting details using different sizes and colors as building blocks. Something as plain as a metal chimney shroud can be interesting if the wood surround is finely detailed and relates to the rest of the house. But more than just in material selection, a chimney's shape should be consistent with the rest of the house exterior. A complicated chimney on a simple cabin would probably look ridiculous, as would a simple chimney on a house with a wide variety of shapes.

No matter what size the house, if columns are used, they should always be consistent with other details and with the whole house.

A chimney is only one exterior detail. There are many others, but whatever is used should make sense with the rest of the exterior. A Greek column on a Craftsman house, for example, would look out of place, as would an elaborately carved wood bracket on a house with steel siding. An exterior rail usually looks best when you can find an equivalent on the interior. No detail stands alone. When you look at the exterior of a house, you should expect all the exterior details to combine gracefully with the larger elements of the house. Continuity is the goal with any detail.

This straightforward chimney is perfectly consistent with this simple cottage design. A more elaborate chimney wouldn't have seemed right.

the personality of home

The physical attributes of the face of home give us a good way of describing (and even designing) a house. But quite apart from the physical characteristics is something more qualitative, more subjective—it's the effect they produce. In a word, it's the house's personality.

Houses can feel austere, inviting, dark, moody, happy, and even exuberant. A house made of stone will generally feel heavier than one made of wood; a house of a dark color more somber than one of a light color. A block house with very few exterior details is likely to feel more austere than one in wood or brick with many and varied details or textures. The way a house looks gives it a certain personality, which in turn evokes a response from anyone who looks at it. If, for instance, a house is built from a single, uninterrupted material such as dark stucco with small window openings and no details, and the exterior is completely symmetrical to boot, the house might feel quite formal, maybe even standoffish. The same house might be completely different in another color and with bigger windows or more elaborate details. An asymmetrical house made up of many shapes with a lot of windows would probably feel more informal. Houses that have prominent, dark roofs and are close to the ground often feel mysterious. The point is that houses, like people, have personalities. Much like faces, some houses can make us smile, while others make us frown.

Our houses are made up of many qualities, physical and emotional. This book is my attempt to show that when we examine their exteriors and look at their details, large and small, we have an opportunity to understand them far more deeply than we ever could by relying on labels. Next time you look at a house, think about all its parts and the influence each has on the other. Many houses today just don't feel real. They lack authenticity. Our times seem to demand a sound bite, one-size-fits-all solution, the quick fix. Labeling our houses seems to fit the bill. But our houses are not advertisements but real places to live, and if we can learn to understand and describe them in a more thoughtful way, we may just be on our way to a more distinctive face of home.

Personality is the collective impact of materials, design, and detailing: A high stone wall with small windows presents a much different face than a low, light–filled connector joining two wings of a house.

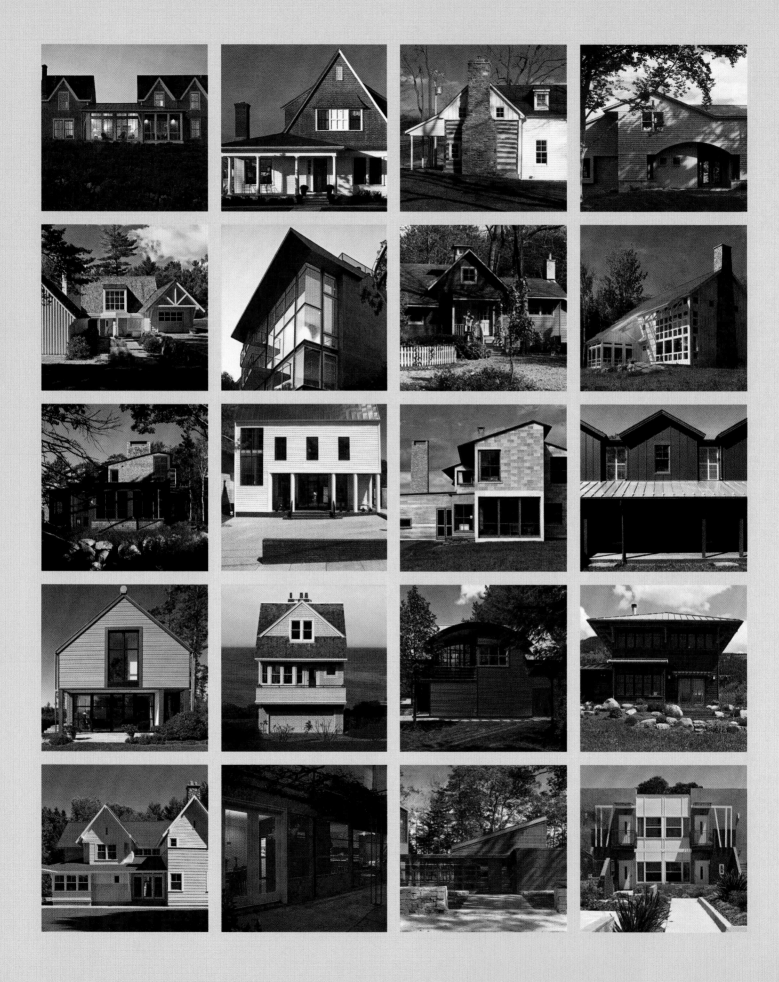

faces of home

northern light

two faces of home

You can tell where some houses are located just by looking at them. I can imagine this house only in a northern climate. The roof and walls tell us that immediately. The broad, sheltering roof suggests that you would be protected from whatever nature throws at you, especially snow. The gable ends of the roof, detailed with board-and-batten siding, cast deep shadows in the low northern light. This house designed by David Salmela in Minnesota can be appreciated on two cultural levels: It has the look and feel of a house that belongs to the northern American Midwest while at the same time evokes the Scandinavian traditions of the region.

As with all good faces, these shapes also give us a read of what we're likely to encounter on the inside of the house. [1] [2] Much of the living/dining/kitchen wing is an exact spatial reflection of the gable. In other words, it's a story-and-a-half space throughout. On the south-facing elevation, large windows, roof dormers, and a series of doors tell us the house is reaching out for the warmth of sunlight. [3] The sparse detailing of the roof dormers makes them look as if they've been peeled out of the roof rather than placed on top of it. [4] That reinforces the sense of roof as one continuous cover—or shelter—over the whole house.

[3]

[4]

On the colder north side of the house, the look is entirely different. Here, there are no doors or dormers, only five small windows spaced rhythmically along the wall. [5] The south elevation is open to the outside, the north quite closed. Even the trusswork, brackets, and overhanging roof on the gable end of the garage wing reinforce the effect of shelter. The detailing adds some life and character, but it also provides a real sense of protection in front of the garage doors, as if to say, "No snow allowed here."

6

7

8

9

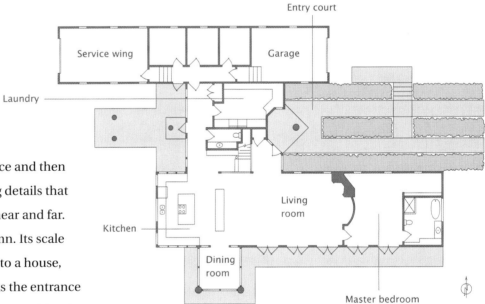

Entry court

Service wing

Garage

Laundry

Living room

Kitchen

Dining room

Master bedroom

Houses should hold your interest from a distance and then again close up. Sometimes houses have striking details that contribute to their exterior interest from both near and far. Here it's a column, but this is no ordinary column. Its scale seems to belong more to a larger building than to a house, yet it works on a number of levels. First, it marks the entrance from a distance. [6] It would be hard to miss the combination of the column and a large dormer above that together say, "Enter here." As you move closer, the column begins to take on a structural significance because it becomes clear that it is holding up the entry roof. [7] [8] And inside, you find a similar, though slightly smaller, version of the column marking the stair to the second floor. [9] This kind of inside-outside recall or repetition of a single element can go a long way toward gluing the experience of the exterior and interior together.

But there's another meaning here, too—a symbolic one. The column was made from a tree cut from the site. And according to Norwegian culture, whose roots found their way into the traditions of northern Minnesota, using a tree from the site has deep significance. Although clearly man-made and refined, the large exterior column reminds us of the house's roots and anchors it to the land.

The same strong gable form is used to define the upper portion of the living space and the sheltering extension of a garage roof.

The choice of materials can reinforce the message that the exterior faces are trying to give us about a house— not unlike the way that fabric in clothing can say something about the shape, size, and gender of the person wearing it. The exterior siding used on the walls of this house is a good example. Extra-wide board-and-batten vertical siding on the gables reinforces their strong, upright shape. The same siding at the base of the house, along with the pronounced eave trim, emphasizes the wall's role in holding up the roof. You could change both gable and wall materials to, say, shingles, but the character of the elevation would change dramatically and the high contrast between roof and wall would be lost.

A dormer and trellis on the west elevation include a simpler version of the column at the formal entry on the opposite side of the house. Both dormer and trellis are visual extensions of the wall siding. They provide a place to sit both inside and out in the late afternoon light—which is so important in this northern climate.

Outside and inside are connected and extended into the landscape through an array of complementary window, siding, and trellis patterns.

The distinctive shape
of the steep gable outside
is a direct expression of the
high-ceilinged living space
inside.

Unique dormers not only mark the location of entries
on the exterior but also provide comfortable spots
inside for sitting in the sun.

a symphony of roofs

room with a view

The first time I saw this house, I couldn't help but think of a tree house. [1][2]
Although the house isn't actually perched in a tree, of course, it almost seems that
way from a distance, one indication of just how well it is connected to its site. In
fact, it's hard to tell where the site ends and the house begins—always the sign of a
well-designed home. [3]

3

4

The house, designed by Van Dam & Renner Architects, rises up from the top of a hill along the Maine coast in colors that match its natural surroundings. It's capped by a striking master bedroom with commanding views of the water. 4 This room seems to pop out of the much larger first floor, which houses living and dining areas, a kitchen, two smaller bedrooms, and an entry. Above these first-floor spaces, two long, low-sloped roofs at right angles to each other work as a counterbalance to the bulk of the master bedroom above. 5 These lower sections of the house seem to hug the site and emphasize the prominence of the lofty bedroom.

The contrast between the high central tower and the roofs over the living spaces below is what gives this house its real drama. At a single glance, the roofs also tell you something about the floor plan inside. It's hard to imagine the first floor as anything other than living spaces or the second floor as anything other than a special room with a special view.

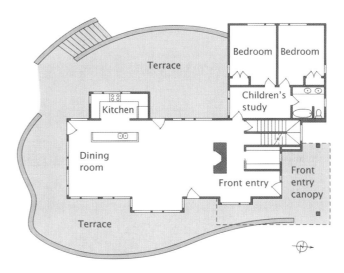

First floor

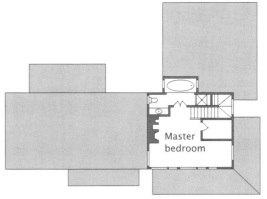

Second floor

7

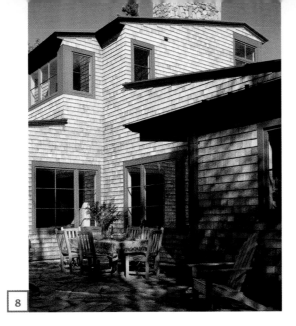

8

While the major roofs help to give the exterior its overall balance, smaller roofs over two bays 6 and a cantilevered entrance enhance the effect. 7 These smaller roof extensions not only have the same pitch as the main roofs but also extend the house outward to a level stone terrace that wraps around the house and provides outdoor space for lounging, dining, or just looking at the water. Because the terrace has both east and west exposures, it makes the outside of the house appealing at different times of the day and even at different times of the year. It accomplishes something else, too. Depending where you are on the terrace, the house takes on a different scale. On the living room side, for example, you sit up against a one-story wall fully exposed to the east and south sun. 6 On the west-facing side just off the kitchen, you sit next to a two-story wall that captures southwest breezes in the summer and partially blocks harsh northeast winds at other times of the year. 8 9 It's a totally different experience on opposite sides of the house.

Color is one of the most underrated tools for achieving harmony, but this house shows how well it can be used. Colors in the natural environment—tree bark, stone, and vegetation— are matched by the stone terrace, foundation, and chimney, the natural shingles on the body of the house, and the darker, complementary colors of windows and trim. The colors of house and site are seen as one, as they should be on any good face of home. 10

9

10

details in stone and glass

Details mean the most when they spring from the whole house and seem to belong to it, bolstering the overall design. It doesn't matter whether the details are on the outside or inside. Here, the positioning, color, and texture of stone reinforces the nature of the house. Stone forms the base of the house, and it's used for retaining walls, terrace floors, and on the chimney, where it not only caps the roofs but also acts as a kind of pinwheel around which the rest of the house seems to spin. Even its texture is appropriate: It's laid up in a somewhat random pattern of various size stones that gives it an appealing connection to the natural landscape around it. You could imagine finding these stones on the site.

Using stone at the foundation and on the chimney at the roof helps connect the house to the colors and materials of the site.

A continuous projecting roof covers both the outside entry porch and a window bay that provides a view of the entry foyer from within.

Windows provide another kind of detailing that seems to flow naturally from the rest of the house. At the entry, for example, a small bay window connects the house with the canopy above. Windows also are used to turn corners at key locations, such as the living room, the master bedroom, and the second-floor bathroom. This detail intensifies the openness of these spaces and strengthens their connection to the outside. That's especially true in the master bedroom and bath, where windows help impart that tree-house quality that drew me to the house in the first place.

Windows placed on walls across from each other allow a clear view through the house to the landscape beyond.

Large, low windows at the second-floor master bedroom and bath give this house a tree-house quality.

straight-faced

bands of walls and windows

"Plan as guide" is an important principle for a good face of home. Typically, that means you can tell what's going on inside the house by looking at the outside: A large window on the first floor says living room, for example, while a much smaller window elsewhere suggests a bathroom. But that doesn't appear to be the case on this house overlooking the Strait of Juan de Fuca in Washington State designed by The Miller Hull Partnership. [1][2] Even from a distance, the alternating bands of wall and windows make it clear that this is no ordinary exterior. [3] Close up, the consistent size and strictly regular placement of windows doesn't seem to tell us much of anything about the inside. Instead, it almost seems as if the architects chose to disregard the plan to focus solely on the exterior. It's a rhythm that works well with the site and the distant evergreens as they march their way to the shoreline, but does it work on the inside?

3

A closer look reveals that the plan really hasn't been disregarded at all; it's just been adjusted to work naturally with this unusual exterior. Each room has an appropriate amount of glass, some more than others, depending on its use and importance. And because most of the house is essentially one room deep, rooms such as the kitchen and dining room have exposures on two sides. [4] The living room and master bedroom have three exposures—to the east, south, and west. Given their importance, that's the way it should be. [5]

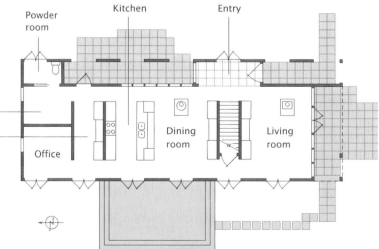

Powder room

Kitchen

Entry

Art room

Mudroom

Office

Dining room

Living room

N

5

4

6

7

8

9

Some of the most interesting houses are those that break the rules in subtle ways while still managing to achieve an overall balance and harmony. As seen with other houses in this book, architects often add wings, bays, and dormers to their designs to accommodate various uses or to achieve a better balance of mass or scale. Here, the architects have done the opposite. Instead of adding, they've subtracted from the body of the house by carving away areas to make outside spaces while maintaining a strong sense of order.

On the southern end of the first floor, the architects have recessed the continuous glass wall of the living room (another way of looking at it is that the second floor has been cantilevered) to create a sitting area protected from sun and rain. 6 7

The architects have used the same approach on the two long sides of the house. Although they may look the same from a distance, the first floor on the east side has actually been set back, just like the south side, to form a covered entry porch with access not only to the front door but also to a number of rooms along the length of the house. 9 Contrast that exterior corridor with the continuous interior corridor on the west side of the house. 8 The architects could have attached a separate entry porch on the east side, but they chose instead not to compromise the strong exterior order and look. Exterior and interior are working in harmony.

details in outline

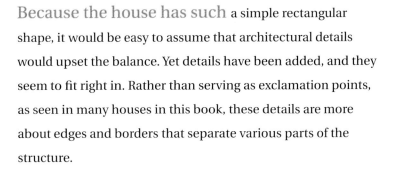

Because the house has such a simple rectangular shape, it would be easy to assume that architectural details would upset the balance. Yet details have been added, and they seem to fit right in. Rather than serving as exclamation points, as seen in many houses in this book, these details are more about edges and borders that separate various parts of the structure.

A compact eave and fascia detail, combined with a staightforward gutter and downspout at all the corners, reinforces the overall simplicity of the house.

The gutters and downspouts on this house are good examples. A minimal eave overhang and compact gutter detail are combined with downspouts at the four corners. Although such functional elements aren't typically thought of as real design details, here they help outline and reinforce the strong, simple shape of the house. The color of the lead-coated copper also blends nicely with the grays and blues of the house. Neither gutter nor downspout stands out, thus reinforcing the overall rhythm of the house rather than interfering with it.

At the peak of the roof, a ridge vent in the same lead-coated copper serves a similar role. In this sometimes harsh environment along the water's edge, providing a ridge vent that ventilates but doesn't leak in wind-driven rain is a common challenge. Instead of trying to hide the detail, the architects have actually made more of it with a strong form that enhances the shape of the house, just as the gutters and downspouts do. One way to imagine how this is working is to take away, in your mind, the walls and roof of the house. What would be left is a framework composed of gutters, downspouts, and the roof vent in the shape of the house.

Even commonplace details such as a chimney top and ridge vent are given enough special attention to enhance their visual role on the exterior of the house.

Windows, doors, and built-in shutters and screens offer a wide variety of options for experiencing the connection between inside and out.

One striking detail on the west wall is invisible most of the day: a series of sliding shutters and screens that fit neatly into pockets in the wall. With the shutters tucked away, the brightly trimmed walls clearly support the house, and the windows and doors can be opened to provide ventilation. When the shutters are closed, they block low afternoon sun and could, if necessary, offer some storm protection. More than any other detail on the house, this one springs naturally from the design as a whole, an indicator of a good face of home.

change of face

reading faces

Faces say a lot about people. Even small changes in expression are clues to what a person is feeling, whether it's joy, amusement, fatigue, or something else. The walls of a house are a big part of the face of home, and just like a human face they offer subtle information about what's going on inside. When the outward face of a house varies from back to front or side to side, it's clear evidence that interior uses are different, too.

5

The west face of this house, designed by my firm, is a good place to start. First, it gives a strong sense of entry. Dominated by two high wings, this wall directs you straight into the house through a trio of glass doors. [1] [2] The entries on so many houses built today seem mostly for show, more like a country club than a house. Large columns, arched windows, and oversized porches shout "entry," but they feel out of scale and off-putting. Not here. This covered entry has a more human scale as it leads to a comfortable and welcoming entry hall.

The back of the house is dramatically different. Its north-facing walls open up with expanses of glass to allow sweeping views of a meadow and old stone walls. [6] The combination living, dining, and kitchen areas on the first floor and the master bedroom dormer above are distinctly different from the more

solid entry wall, even though they clearly come from the same family of shapes and materials. The design tells us these rooms and their views are an essential part of the house. They seem even more magical at night. [3] [4]

Moving around the house, the walls of the guest bedroom wing have their own look and feel. [5] This side seems almost separate from the main body of the house—just as a guest room should. Even the garage, the most utilitarian of structures, uses elements from the rest of the house to support its own identity. A bit like a yoyo on a string, it is tentatively attached by a covered walk to the house.

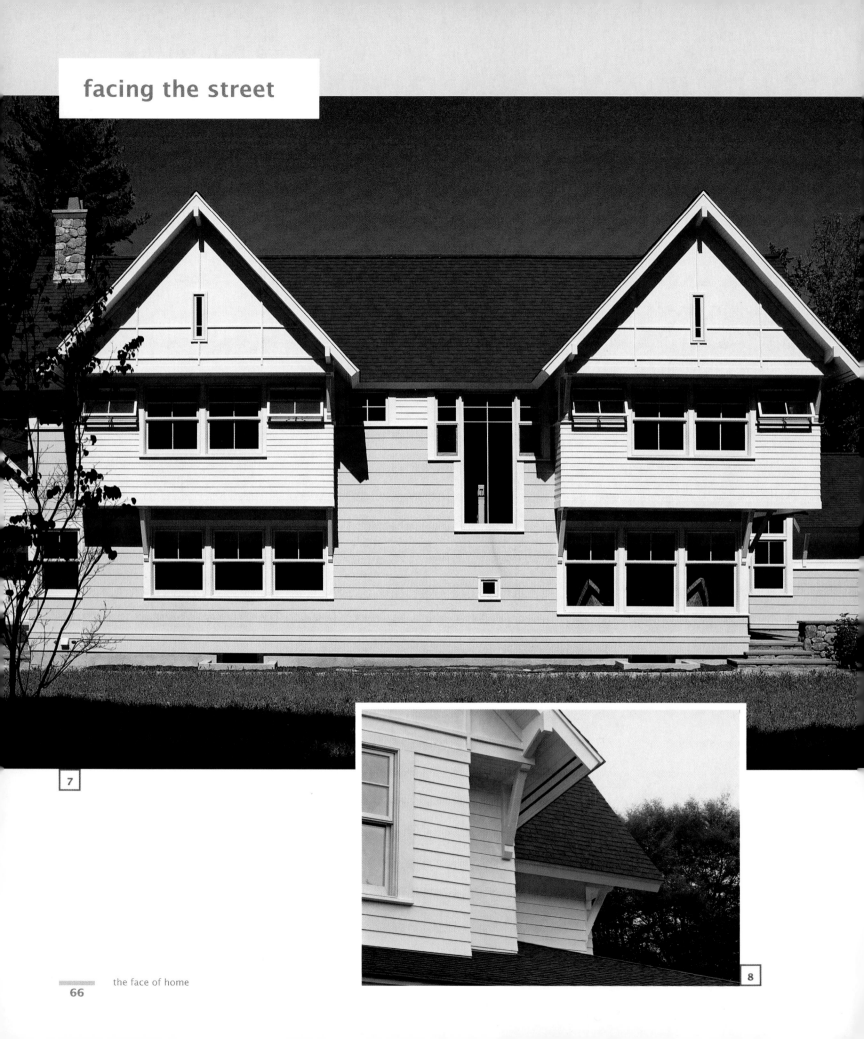

7

8

9

10

Around the front of the house, the walls that face the street send their own message. The two children's bedrooms on the second floor are cantilevered twice over the rooms below, setting them apart from the main body of the house 7 (imagine that wall as one flat plane, and you'll see how the cantilevers add visual appeal). The bedrooms are made even more prominent by changes in color and materials.

Additional layers of detail help to enhance the effect. The cantilevered sections of these dormers get their own supporting brackets, providing a sense of structural support as well as visual interest. 8 Also, each portion of overhang is made from its own material: one with clapboard, one with decorative board and batten, and one with tongue-and-groove siding. 9 These same ideas are carried to other parts of the house, such as the garage. 10

Vertical slot windows at the center of the bedroom dormers not only add more detail but also prevent glare on the cathedral portion of the room by minimizing sharp contrasts in interior light. 11 Like all good details, these narrow windows have both a functional purpose and an aesthetic expression. Another small window, just below the larger main stair window on the street side, lets just the right amount of light into the basement stair. 9

11

enter with a twist

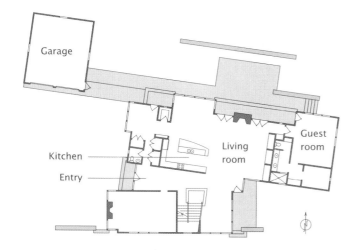

Garage

Kitchen

Entry

Living room

Guest room

As you move back to the west side, it's apparent once inside the house that the entry is wedge shaped. It's formed by a slight twist of the full two-story wing to the right so the wing parallels the street while the main body of the house remains parallel to the backyard for better views. The result is an entry hall that seems welcoming, with a wide space near the front door.

This wedge is really the glue that holds the plan together. It extends from the formal entry door to the opposite side of the house and acts as a connector between the front and back wings of the house on the first floor. The entry's herringbone floor pattern distinguishes it from the other floors in the house. Across the entry hall, a bridge on the second floor connects the children's wing to the master bedroom wing.

The entry hall also contains the stairway to the second floor; you're given a hint of the stair on the exterior by the tall window that faces the street. As with the exterior walls, the stair also has multiple layers of detail. Balusters are separated from the treads and handrails with metal spacers, and like the wings of the house, they are given a slight twist. Even the stair newels are out of the ordinary. Each has its own lantern that serves as a beacon as you make your way from one floor to the other.

The wedge-shaped entry hall running the length of the house provides views to the outside, connects all the spaces on the first floor, and accommodates the stair to the second floor.

The unique stair with its large landing, lantern newels, finely detailed balusters, and oversized windows serves as a pivotal point in the plan.

light and solid

the private face

A building lot surrounded by other houses poses design challenges you wouldn't encounter in a more private setting. To take full advantage of the site, the plan must balance the need for views with the need for privacy while taking into account the proximity of neighbors and the street. It's especially difficult when the house is built on a small, steep site, as is the case with this Los Angeles home designed by Steven Ehrlich Architects. [1][2]

In such a situation, a typical response might be to make a solid house wall at the street, and that's almost what's done here—but not quite. By using high and low walls and the garage as a screen, Ehrlich has created a private front yard, a kind of inner court. This approach is far different from those used for many of the other houses in this book because the first thing you notice as you come near is a wall, not a part of the house itself. Only the upper part of the house peeks over the wall and into the street.

After you pass through a door in the front wall, [3] a new world opens up, one with majestic views of Los Angeles and the surrounding area clear through the house. From the inner court, you have access to the house and to a deck over the garage. [4] You can also go down the sloping site to the lower floor of the house. This inner courtyard, with indigenous plantings and stone slabs [5] that almost seem to float above the ground, is a natural substitute for a generous terrace or deck that would have been difficult to build off the back on such a steep site. [6]

3

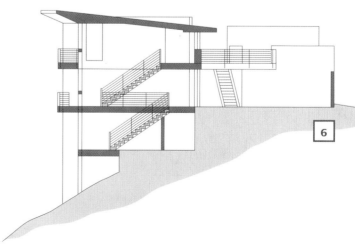

6

8

7

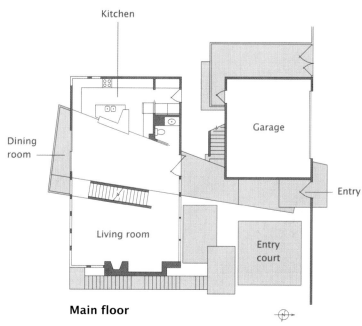

9

Main floor

While the glass walls are the main attraction, the solid walls at the sides of the house are not without interest. Most of the lower portions of the sidewalls are not even visible because they act as retaining walls and anchors to the slope. But even on the upper floors where they can be seen, the walls are mostly windowless because the architect has used various elements of the house to screen views to and from neighbors on both sides. For instance, on one side of the house solid walls of the mudroom near the garage entrance and tall storage cabinets in the kitchen block views of the interior from outside. On the other side of the house, a three-story stucco wall not only provides the same kind of screening but also serves as a visual mooring for the rest of the house. 7 With all that glass, the house might otherwise feel too light. This is a great example of a house exterior that accurately reflects a practical need, in this case the need for privacy.

Solid walls give way to windows on the back side. Here, glass capped by a dramatic hatlike roof is the prominent material, allowing spectacular views in a 180-degree sweep. 8 The only elements that break the sweep are two small balconies, one off the dining area and another off the master bedroom, whose angled shape seems to reinforce the sweeping panoramas they provide. This wall has a message, too: All that glass speaks to the importance of views from the kitchen, dining room, living room, and master bedroom. The glass even turns the corner at the rear of the house without any corner framing, a detail that permits a more unobstructed view from inside. The subtle change in the glass framing also helps define the two-story living space and stair within, a central feature of the house. 9

For all the house's solidness, its personality is really about lightness. More than simply the amount of glass that's been used, this quality comes from the way the details of the house are put together. The delicate window mullions are a good example. Given the wind exposure on the site, they might have been thicker or there might have been more of them. Instead, their thinness contributes to better views from within and an overall sense of lightness. The roof has the same effect. It hangs out over the glass and extends beyond the solid sidewalls like the brim of a hat. Had the roof edge been flush with the walls below, the house would have seemed more monolithic. Even the smooth-textured exterior stucco wall panels contribute to the feeling of lightness— they don't seem as heavy as they might have been if made of brick or even wood.

Inside, the white plaster walls and the steel stair with open risers seem suspended in space, while stainless-steel cables on the stair and outside balconies once again reinforce the personality of lightness (see the photo on the facing page). No single material or detail gives a house its personality. It's always the combination of parts. In this case, what at first glance seems like a solid house from the street or from next door turns out to be very different once you've seen all four faces.

Perched on a hill, this house provides spectacular views of the Los Angeles skyline while providing privacy from the street and neighbors.

A subtle distinction of parts and materials at all scales from the roof overhang down to exterior siding joints contributes to the overall sense of lightness.

two-faced neighbor

opposites attract

When people describe houses, they tend to think in absolute terms, using labels that don't always completely fit. One of the standard chants, for example, is that a house is either contemporary or traditional. Truth is, houses are hardly ever wholly one thing. Well-designed houses are often a mix of styles because following one style to the exclusion of all other possibilities can lead to a sterile, predetermined look—a house in a particular style, yes, but one with no real style of its own.

3

This house in Chevy Chase, Maryland, designed by architect Robert Gurney, mixes the seemingly conflicting pulls of contemporary and traditional styles very well and achieves a look that's all its own. Most houses in this neighborhood have steep roofs with large overhangs, double-hung windows divided into small panes, porches that face the street, and white siding and trim. ⬚3 On the sides that face the street, Gurney has played off those elements without mimicking them (there's no real roof overhang, for instance) to create a house that fits in but also stands out.

But the most striking thing about the house is the dramatic contrast between front and back. Most Americans use their backyards as private domains while treating front yards as more public spaces. This house deals with those two different attitudes in an interesting way. In front, the house respects the historic character and scale of the street, ⬚4 but in back the language is looser, responding more directly to the homeowner's functional needs with hardly any reference to the surrounding neighbors. ⬚5

First floor

Kitchen

Living room

Dining room

Entry porch

Lap pool

a different story around the back

Most of the family activity takes place in the back, and there's nothing restrained about this part of the house. The back half seems to be bursting out all over with different shapes and materials. For example, a curved exterior wall on the second floor, clad in lead-coated copper sheets, contains the children's bath and helps connect the front half of the house to the back. 6 That same copper cladding is used on a small rectangular bumpout that houses the water closet in the master bathroom. 7 The roof over the front portion of the house also is clad in metal, providing some continuity of materials between front and back. On the other hand, most of the master bedroom has vertical wood siding stained dark, a real departure from the front siding of horizontal white clapboards. Even the windows of the master bedroom have a lot of variety. Some are clear glass while others are translucent plastic panels that allow southern light in but preserve privacy.

7

The most distinctive elements on the south side are a tall chimney and a one-story pavilion-like bay just off the kitchen and dining area that serves as a circulation area between inside and out. 8 9 These two elements, the chimney in concrete block and the bay of all glass with its own small, flat roof trimmed in lead-coated copper, make an interesting pair. The chimney, solid and tall, acts like an anchor for the bay. They're in balance, as elements of a good face of home should be.

8

9

In contrast to many handicap-accessible ramps, this one is barely noticeable and provides gracious access to the front door.

There's another reason why this house is far from ordinary: One of the children who lives here uses a wheelchair. Accordingly, the house includes wide-open halls, subtle ramps, and level access to both the front and rear of the house, including the pool. From the street, you'd hardly notice the wheelchair-accessible ramp. The only hint it's there is a change in angle of a low brick wall. At the front entry door, there's no difference in height between the covered porch floor and the generous entry hall floor beyond. At the entry hall, an elevator provides access to both upper floors. This unobstructed flow continues from the entry hall down a wide, light-filled corridor, where once again there is no height difference between the inside wood floor and the outside terrace. Doors also are unusually wide, and the large amount of glass leaves the impression that inside and outside are one.

One of the serious design problems of our time is that accessibility is often treated as a separate design issue rather than as an integral part of the overall design. This house manages to be both accessible and beautiful. It's not just a house that's wheelchair friendly but also a study in contrasts of public and private, front yard and backyard, neighborhood friendly and totally unique, where seeming opposites really attract.

A glass-filled front entry hall is a welcoming gesture to the neighbors and gives a hint of the unique backyard beyond.

A wide, brightly lit corridor connects the front and back of the house and provides uninterrupted access between the interior and exterior along the length of the terrace and pool.

the shoebox challenge

building a better shoebox

Some sites don't give you a lot of room to maneuver, and increasingly tight zoning regulations can make it even harder to design a house. Regulations, in fact, can become the basis of design. Such was the risk when my firm designed this house in southern Maine for a lot measuring barely 6,000 sq. ft. Setback restrictions dictated the width, length, and even the maximum height of the building. [1] [2] Our challenge was to find a way to keep the house from looking like a shoebox.

Once all the regulations had been taken into account, we were left with a house that could be no larger than 20 ft. wide, 65 ft. long, and 35 ft. high. All the living space, including outside decks and even the roof overhangs, had to fit within those dimensions. Rather than looking at these requirements as insurmountable restraints on design, we responded by dealing with each face of the house separately.

On the two short ends of the house, where privacy is not a concern, we included a generous number of windows and doors. Overhanging decks provide intimate places for conversation, coffee, or taking in spectacular ocean views. [3] [4] A small extended roof on the kitchen side provides shade for that deck, while upper and lower decks on the living room side are perfect for sitting in the sun. The long sides of the house, which face neighboring houses, had to be very different. On the southeast side, the neighbor is only about 20 ft. away, so that face is somewhat stark. [6] On the opposite side, there's a neighboring house at one end of the lot, so there, too, the face is somewhat closed for privacy. But as you move away from the neighboring house, this side changes dramatically, opening up with large windows and stunning views. [5]

5

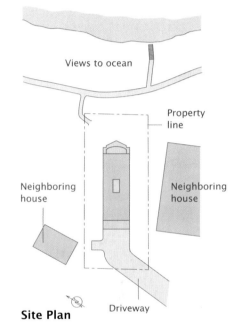

Views to ocean

Property line

Neighboring house

Neighboring house

Driveway

Site Plan

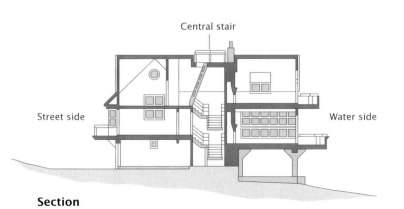

Central stair

Street side

Water side

Section

6

the shoebox challenge

liftoff

8

This house is raised off the ground to provide space for a garage on the street side and boat storage on the water side (and, of course, the added height gives most of the rooms better views). 7 But one of the difficult things about a long, narrow house that's been lifted off the ground is how to get around inside. We eliminated corridors by placing the stair in the center of the house and freeing up both ends for larger rooms. 8 The stair, or more precisely the source of natural light for the stair, becomes a prominent feature on the outside of the house, too. Light enters through tall, vertical windows and a long row of small, horizontal windows just below the roof edge at the center of the house. On the inside, the windows provide great views of the water at every level. 9

Another challenge with a house that's raised off the ground is making it feel as if it still belongs to the site, rather than hovering over it. Our solution was to anchor the house in the back with the solid feel of the enclosed garage while opening the side facing the water and resting it on two support columns. 10 11 The result is a house that is both anchored to the shoreline and perched over the water's edge, just the right character for its beachfront location.

In spite of some very confining site regulations, the variety in siding materials, trim, and window types keeps this house from looking like a box.

On most houses you can add a porch or overhang to prevent a boxy appearance, but we were limited here. Porches and decks on the short ends of the house help, but we also introduced changes in materials and ribbonlike horizontal details on each floor to help alleviate the shoebox look (see the photo at left). Tightly spaced vertical siding on the lower floor acts as a base on which the main living area sits. On the next level, horizontal clapboards accentuate the length of the house and keep it from looking quite so tall. The upper bedroom floor is sheathed in wood shingles, the same material as the roof, which helps to give it a hatlike quality that nicely finishes out the house. Good houses, in fact, often have a three-part theme of base, middle, and roof, much like the legs, torso, and head of a human body. With such an arrangement, the main body of the house has a better relationship to the site and the sky by having a base to sit on and a roof to top it off.

Each side of the house responds to its immediate surroundings by opening up with windows and doors when privacy is not an issue and presenting a more solid wall when it is.

Subtle, ribbonlike details that include a "belt coursing" between the two living floors and a "water table" at the top of the base are no more than a few inches thick and high, but they serve to tie the various materials and house together around all four faces. The variously sized windows are composed mostly of the same square pattern. They add texture and interest, like the rest of the house detailing, and they show how important even the smallest of touches can be in creating a good face of home.

By eliminating long corridors along the sides of the house, rooms at both ends are the full width of the allowable footprint (20 ft.).

house in garden

a long, narrow lot

We often think of house and garden as separate entities, but in this southern California home they are intimately connected. [1][2] Designed around the efficient use of outdoor space, the house was almost completely enveloped by plantings a few years after it was built. [3] That was not an unintended outcome but a testament to good siting, a thoughtful plan, and details that support the relationship between house and garden.

3

Architects Koning Eizenberg of Santa Monica made two important decisions about the lot, which measures 167 ft. long and just 50 ft. wide. First, instead of placing the house squarely in the middle, they placed it to one side, just a few feet from the lot line. They also placed the house closer to one end of the lot than the other, even though there was street access at both ends. Those two decisions provide enormous benefits for the homeowners and the way they use the outside. Instead of having two narrow and unusable side yards, they have one big yard running the whole length of the house. [4][5][6] Placing the house closer to one street provides more usable yard and also defines one end of the lot as informal and the other as formal. At the informal end, a carport and workshop act as a screen and gateway for the family entry. At the other end, an opening in the shrubs and trees provides privacy and allows access to the formal entry of the house. [7]

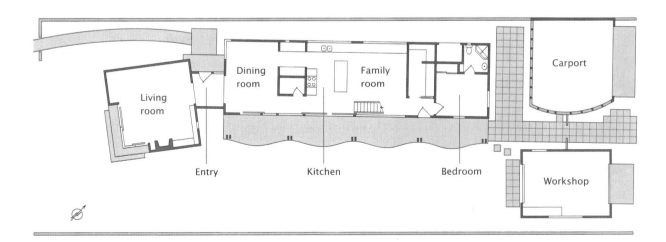

4

5

6

7

wall of glass

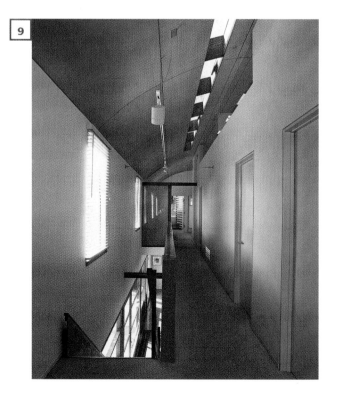

Decisions about a site always have an impact on how a house looks on the outside. The most prominent elevation of this house is the one that faces the yard. Except for a guest bedroom at the end, this wall is almost all glass. At first glance, the space behind the glass seems like a long corridor 8 , but it's actually a free-flowing space that connects all the rooms of a very open plan. As a result, the kitchen, dining, and family rooms have a clear view to the garden outside. It's interesting to compare that space with the corridor on the second floor. There, a long hallway also connects the rooms (in this case, bedrooms), but because of the need for more privacy the space is not as open. 9 The architects have signaled that by using four much smaller windows along the length of the wall. The middle bedroom gets south light through high transoms and a long, thin skylight in the curved roof, a detail that provides both light and privacy.

The continuous glass wall on the first floor might have been enough to create a close relationship between the house and garden, but the architects didn't stop there. They added an abundantly planted metal trellis that provides an exterior circulation path. 10 It also serves as a hard-surfaced, transitional area for shaded sitting that's a nice contrast to the more sun-drenched areas of the yard. One of the most interesting details of this long wall is the way the horizontal glass mullions reinforce the horizontal nature of the house itself. The glass slides open at the informal kitchen/family area to provide a large opening to the outside. Contrast that opening with the more restrained double doors at the dining room, which provide just a bit more privacy. 11

The balance between openness and screening, between public and private, is an important feature of this house, and it's nicely illustrated by the pavilion-like living room at the west end of the site. Twisted slightly out of line with the rest of the house and with windows only at the southernmost corner (see the plan on p. 96), the living room looks almost as if it has turned its back on the main body of the house and side yard. But the decision to turn this room away actually helped create two yards—the one big, open side yard and a more intimate yard off the living room. The twist is also just enough to provide a larger, more accommodating formal entry. When you have a small lot, subtle design tweaks like these can help you squeeze every advantage out of the available space.

Because of the placement of the windows, the formal living room (above) and the master bedroom (at right) each have their own unique views and feel.

Screening for privacy or to provide shade is accommodated in a variety of ways, from simple window shades to more elaborate wood slats at the formal entry.

On the second floor, what was originally a studio over the living room is now part of the master suite. It's not hard to see why. Surrounded almost entirely by glass and capped by an overhanging roof to help shade the sun, it's reminiscent of an old-fashioned sleeping porch. Views above the trees to the surrounding neighborhood are tempered by delicate window shades. This is an interesting contrast to the living room below with its limited views of the neighborhood and expansive views to the garden. Each one of these rooms has its own unique views, each is reflected on the exterior face, and each demonstrates again how to use a small lot effectively.

The idea of screening also is evident in some of the smaller details of the house. The tightly spaced horizontal slats at the formal entry allow light into the hall but screen views to the family yard beyond. An outdoor fireplace screen, about the height of the first floor, has a dual purpose—screening the area in front of it from neighbors but also protecting the plants behind it from heat and embers. Along with a low concrete-block wall, the screen creates a small but wonderful outdoor room for year-round family use. The ability to fulfill both a practical purpose and an aesthetic one is the mark of any good detail on the face of home.

A comfortable outdoor room is created for year-round use by combining the fireplace and a high metal shield. The result is a detail that has both functional and aesthetic appeal.

built over time

adding on

Most of the houses in this book were designed and built in an uninterrupted flow that could be measured in months, a process that fixed their identities at one moment in time. But what happens to the face of home when additions are made to the original building over a long period? Houses built over time can have an entirely different appeal, one that stems from a gradual evolution to meet changing needs and circumstances.

3

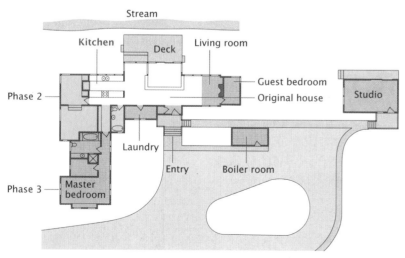

As with many old New England farmhouses, it's hard to know exactly where this house in Woodstock, New York, began or where it might end, but it has a comfortable, mature sense to it. ⊡ As each new part was added, it was given its own identity with paint color or changing rooflines or an individual room shape. There's nothing grand or swaggering about it, but it's the kind of house where most of us would feel right at home. ⊡

Lester Walker, the owner-architect who designed it, has lived here for almost 25 years, and the house's physical appearance can be traced to changes in his life as he went from being a single father to a second marriage with a new child and then middle age. Although room functions have changed over the years, the dining room with a loft/study above and the original living room with its glass ceiling still command a real presence on both the outside and the inside. ⊡ ⊡ ⊡ Elsewhere, the former master bedroom was enlarged to make a new living space and a tiny guest room, the kitchen was modified, and another child's bedroom was added. The central portion of the back side facing a river remains the visual heart of the house, proving that what starts as a good design retains its strength.

4

5

As Walker added to the house, he made sure that each new piece was comfortably scaled to what was already there. For example, at one end of an addition, he added a slightly oversized closet and bathroom as a visual counterweight to the old part of the house. ⬚5⬚ On the side of the house facing the driveway, he used a small sitting bay at the end of the master bedroom to break down the scale of that elevation and make it seem more comfortable. ⬚6⬚

Moving to the other side of the house, the tiny guest bedroom added to the end of the enlarged living room is a shape that doesn't overwhelm what was already there. ⬚7⬚ Walker could have continued the living room gable roof out over the guest bedroom. Instead, he chose to use a shed roof that runs perpendicular to the living room wall. This design decision not only allows more of the new living room chimney to be exposed but also sets the guest room apart from the body of the main house. As in all good elevations, the exterior reflects what's going on inside.

6

7

There's also a smaller-scale version of this kind of move around the front where a new laundry and an old bath were connected to the master bedroom addition. 8 Each space is given its own sense of place and proportion by simply offsetting their roofs.

8

9

Among the most pleasing features of this house are the entries. There are four, and each seems to have just the right amount of detail. The understated main entry has all the right ingredients to let you know it's where you enter the house. A shed roof with wood columns forms a porch to protect the door. The back wall of the porch is a different material than the body of the house, and the ceiling just above the wall has exposed rafters. These material choices, along with a light color for both wall and door, give the whole area an inviting niche-like quality.

The main entry porch is distinguished from the other entries visible from the street by a change in material and color on the back wall.

By using a smaller porch, thinner columns, and a modest gable roof, the master bedroom entry has its own character and scale.

Stark, but nonetheless appropriate, detailing helps define the more functional studio and boiler shed entries.

The separate studio has its own unique entry. The detailing and colors are similar to those at the main entry but on a smaller scale. The small gable roof over the studio entry echoes the large house gable, and the porch columns are thinner than on the main entry. This reduction in scale is also evident at the separate master bedroom entry just to the left of the main entry. As a result, there's no confusing it with the main entry.

The novel boiler shed entry is designed with the same door and colors as the other entries, but there's no attempt to mark its importance with a gable or columns. A small, overhanging roof soffit, just big enough to keep off the rain and snow, gives a hint of its utilitarian nature. A nice final touch is the main entry path light. Originally a birdhouse, even it found a new life over the years.

A former birdhouse, similar in details to the rest of the house, was given a new life as an entry path light.

breaking symmetry

the joy of asymmetry

There's not much mystery in a house that's completely symmetrical: The unerring alignment of elements such as windows and doors makes it obvious how its exterior elevations are organized. But what if various parts of a house are not perfectly aligned and balanced, and what if materials include a mix of textures, shapes, and colors? What you would have is order based on asymmetry, which in the right hands, as this house in Sharon, Connecticut, proves, can be an equally powerful design tool. [1][2]

3

This house is all about overlapping materials and parts arranged in an asymmetrical order that may not be obvious at first. Architect Peter Rose used block, brick, concrete, wood, and metal to define different parts of the house even as they contribute to a pleasing overall composition. The block portions of the house, taller in height and higher on the site, suggest a traditional saltbox design. [3] These areas house informal spaces on the first floor and bedrooms on the second. Wood-clad portions of the building, slightly lower on the site and with a more contemporary feel, contain more formal living and dining spaces and a small private study. On the southwest corner, Rose carved away a corner of the house to create a screened porch, then right next to it added a protruding bay. Although two entirely different shapes, these informal sitting areas are filled with light and offer an intimate connection with the landscape. [4]

On the west side, a small stone wall creates a formal lawn where once there was meadow. Landscape architect Dan Kiley planted a row of maples that shield the house from late afternoon sun, and together these trees and lawn make a kind of outdoor room that can be enjoyed at all times of the year. [5][6]

4

5

6

east-face focus

7

8   9

The east-facing side of the house is particularly successful in its use of different materials and shapes to compose a pleasing whole. There's no perfectly aligned order here. Instead, it's a kit of parts, made up of windows, block, concrete lintels, and recesses and protrusions thoughtfully placed on the outside to help us understand what's happening on the inside. 8 For instance, the recess at the right end of this side 7 is an informal back entry whose overhang offers protection from the weather. Above it, on the second floor, a small shape juts out from the house. 9 It may look a little odd until you realize that its two doors create a private sitting balcony for the master bedroom. Its appearance, too, is a clue to its use.

The same applies to the bay to the left on the first floor. 10 11 Tall, almost floor-to-ceiling double-hung windows provide a clear opening for the morning light to flood the kitchen within. All of these elements, whether they recede or project, are a direct reflection of what's going on inside the house. And that's the sign of a good face of home.

split down the middle

This house achieves a pleasing balance of parts through the use of a wide variety of materials: gravel, concrete, block, brick, wood, and glass.

A light-filled corridor that runs the length of the house (above and facing page) separates the formal and informal spaces on the first floor and includes a stair to bedrooms on the second.

The house is really two one-room-deep houses tied together along an east-west corridor. This divide runs right through the house, serving as a connection between the formal and informal spaces of the first floor and as access to the second floor. Splitting the house like this brings in better light to the first floor, as well as better views and ventilation on the second. The split is clear on the exterior, especially on the north and south faces. Architect Rose has even reinforced the split by carrying a concrete wall from outside, at the formal entrance area on the north side, along the edge of the long hallway inside.

There's another kit of parts at work here, too—the overall site plan. House, studio, and guesthouse, grouped around two gravel courtyards, have a distinctly different feel but still come from the same palette of materials. The guesthouse, for instance, has the same cutaway corners and wood windows as the main house, but its walls are made of raw cement board, a sort of second cousin to the block and concrete of the house.

With a similar palette of materials, the guesthouse has the same look and feel as the main house.

To garage

Back entry

To guest house

Main entry

Screened porch

Kitchen

Sitting room

Study   Living room   Dining room

Main floor

craftsman companion

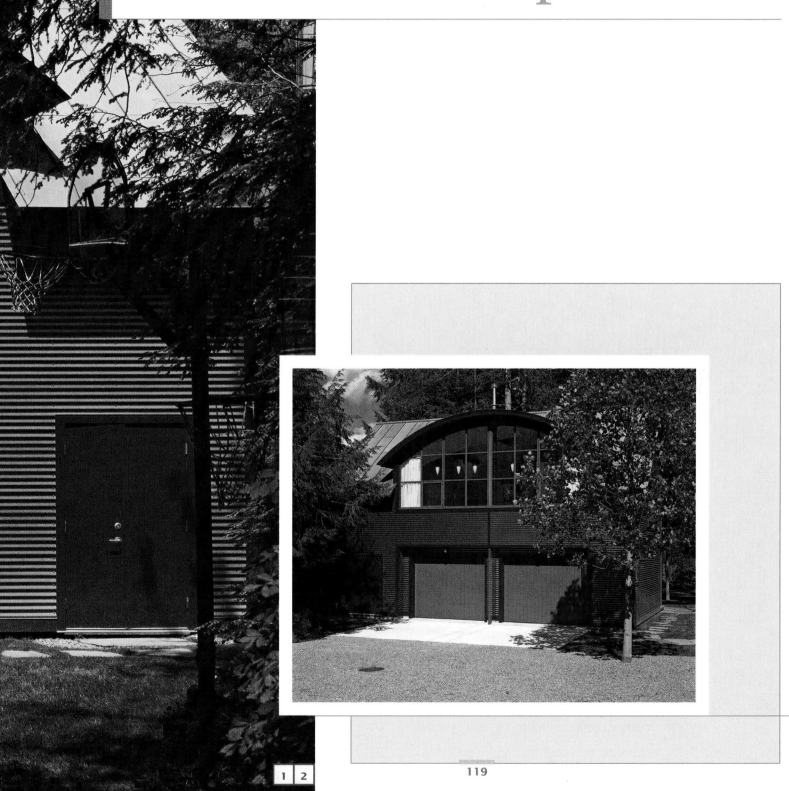

reinventing the craftsman style

Asked to design a garage or guesthouse for a 1910 Craftsman-style house, most of us would probably come up with something that mimicked the features of the original. How could you go wrong? Houses in that style had a warmth, charm, and attention to detail that are still deeply admired. Yet faced with that exact assignment at a house in western Massachusetts, architects Andrus Burr and Ann McCallum did something entirely different. Instead of copying the main house in shape, color, or materials, they reinvented the Craftsman style with a modern interpretation that uses contemporary materials and detailing and bold color. [1]

3

Even from the end of the drive, it's clear that the garage/guesthouse is not an offspring of the main house as much as it is a distant cousin. [3] Nonetheless, there's a similar Craftsman calmness about it, accentuated by a gently curving main dormer completely filled with windows that's reminiscent of an old-fashioned carriage barn. [2] The bold contrast between the red corrugated siding of the garage/guesthouse [6] and the more subdued green of the main house might at first seem glaring. But a subtle use of color helps it work on more than one level. Green and red, of course, are complementary colors. Touches of the red have been used in the window sash in the main house, while the gray/blue of the house trim is repeated on the garage doors and metal window frames. [4] [5] Despite the obvious differences between the two buildings, nothing seems out of place.

This contemporary interpretation is especially effective because it shows that "Craftsman" need not be limited to certain materials or a certain historical era. That's where relying on labels alone can be so misleading. Craftsman, after all, was really about paying keen attention to details in wood, such as siding, windows, and roof edges. That's just what the architects have done here, only with different materials.

4

5

6

state of independence

7

8

What's so interesting about this garage/guesthouse is that it could stand on its own as an independent structure just as well as it complements the main house. You could easily imagine it in a field or on a lake with no other houses around. There's a balance here between dependence and independence that's not always easy to achieve with accessory structures. If you owned the house, you'd have to park the cars, store the garden equipment, and put out the trash—that's where the garage part of this building comes into play. But you'd also want to provide your guests with a comfortable and private retreat of their own. This garage/guesthouse fulfills both roles.

This little building has some unique features as a temporary living place. Looking around the back, we can see that the curved roof is continued all the way through the upper story from the driveway side of the building. This gives guests expansive views in both directions, especially to a large, private yard in the back. A small sitting porch has been carved out of the corner of the dormer out back, which allows guests to sit in the shade and enjoy the yard or get a glimpse of the main house. 7 8 10 Compare the simple gable end facing the main house with the more prominent curved dormer. It's almost as if someone had turned his face away in a gesture of privacy to show only the side of his head. 9

The main feature of the carriage house, a curved ceiling that runs continuously from front entry to back yard, provides tree-top views in both directions.

One of the most common misconceptions about house exteriors is that they are separate from the rest of the design, that they somehow can be applied independently. Architectural labels tend to reinforce that belief because they deal mostly with the exterior look and feel of the house and not with the floor plans. The simple but novel plan of this design shows clearly why inside and outside are integrally related.

The most prominent exterior feature is the glass-filled, curved dormer facing the driveway, but its presence is equally prominent on the interior. The roof shape is completely exposed over the living space on the second floor. The architects could have stopped there and the space would have been interesting enough, but they went further. The curved shapes are reflected in the walls of the porch and in the tile floor, and they help to create a dramatic intersection of rooflines in the ceiling. The exposed intersection of the two roofs also helps define living areas for sitting, sleeping, and porch. Two exposed steel beams, acting as collar ties for the gable roof, are consistent with the metal siding. The wall of the recessed porch along with the bathroom wall on the opposite side define an alcove for the bed.

This finely crafted combination of outside elements and their interior counterparts in a functional plan is another example of how site, plan, and elevations can work in harmony to create a distinctive face of home.

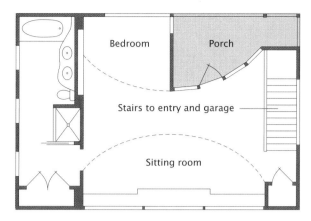

Main floor

Different functional areas of the plan are given definition by the intersection of the curved ceiling and the gable roof.

see-through house

a compound of buildings

There's no rule that says a house has to have just four walls or that it must be composed of a single building. When a house is a collection of individual spaces, each under its own roof, it's called a compound plan. This house in coastal Maine is an example of the compound approach to design. [1][2] Here, activities are spread over three buildings—one for common living areas, another for bedrooms [3], and a third for the garage. [4] It's one thing to achieve a compelling face of home with a single building, but it becomes more complicated when you multiply the number of individual structures.

3

4

Any well-designed house should have a natural relationship with the site; site and house should feel like one. When the house is made up of three buildings, the same principle applies. In addition, each of its parts should be balanced with the others. Think of three entirely different buildings grouped closely together but with little in common. That's what a compound plan has to avoid.

Here, architects Elliott Elliott Norelius have achieved an overall harmony in a number of ways. Most important, the buildings are all relatively low [5], which is easier to achieve with a compound plan because the functions are separated rather than combined into one building. If all of the living activities had been located in a single building, a much taller structure would have resulted. From a distance, the site and the compound of three buildings fit nicely together. Each has a pleasing intimacy and scale. The two-story bedroom wing is balanced on each side by one-story wings. [6]

5

6

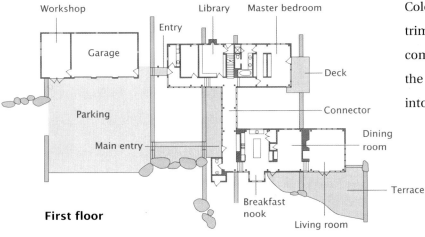

First floor

Workshop

Garage

Parking

Main entry

Entry

Library   Master bedroom

Deck

Connector

Dining room

Terrace

Breakfast nook

Living room

Color also helps unify separate buildings. Natural wood trim, blue-gray shingles, copper cladding, and stone make a complementary palette that seems perfectly appropriate for the Maine setting. Viewed from afar, the compound blends into the surrounding landscape.

7

8

Unlike most houses, where corridors between rooms are inside, a house with a compound plan typically includes some kind of exterior connector. This house has two, one with a roof but no walls to link the garage to the bedroom building [7] and another that's fully enclosed between the bedroom wing and the living wing that houses the kitchen, living room, and other common spaces. [8] What's appealing about both connectors is their transparency—you can see right through them. This effect enhances the separation of the wings, allowing you to see many of the other faces of the compound and the spaces between buildings at the same time. The scale is right, too: The connectors aren't very tall, not much taller than the entry door itself.

The glass connector is also nicely detailed. The walls, consisting mostly of windows, are actually separated from the columns that support the roof. [11] This is a bit like separating the skin from the bones of a house, resulting in a lighter quality than would be possible if much heavier window frames were supporting the roof. Now compare the transparent, open connectors with some of the other appendages on the house, such as the copper-clad enclosures for the entry half-bath [9] and the breakfast nook just around the corner. [10] In terms of openness and materials, the two couldn't be more different, yet it is just that difference in shape, materials, and textures that adds interest and helps to keep the exterior composition of parts in balance.

The greater a number of faces in a compound plan typically means there are more windows and a more free-flowing relationship between inside and out.

A compound house is about more than just its connectors, of course. It's also about the quality of the spaces within and the way they relate to the exterior. The window detailing and openness of the connectors carry through to other parts of the house, such as the living room and the master bedroom. Here, the same kind of window treatment increases the amount of light that flows into those spaces and enhances their relationship to outside decks and terraces.

Like the balance of solid wall and open glass seen at the entry, the south-facing walls of the living and bedroom wings achieve balance through the use of unique detailing. On the second floor of the bedroom wing, small, operable windows allow framed views from three of the four bedrooms. These windows are juxtaposed against a large window at the last bedroom at the end. This larger window tells us from the exterior that this particular room is special. Here, it is a guest bedroom.

Continuous bands of horizontal wood screening run across the upper fixed windows of all four bedrooms, helping to temper the summer sun. The same kind of screened window is used along the entire length of the living wing, allowing dappled southern light into the living, dining, and kitchen spaces. (The shed shape of the roof makes this detail possible because the highest end faces south.) The screening also complements the horizontal shadow lines produced by the exterior shingles. This is another example of allowing details to spring from the whole, a sign of any good face of home.

The exterior glass wall, structural column, and stair are all independent of each other, which gives this connector between buildings a light and open quality.

production perfect

breaking the mold

Built with no particular buyer in mind, the "spec" house is one of the most difficult of all houses to design. Spec houses are production houses, built by contractors or developers for a mass market, which means that the architect—if one is involved— has little room for innovative design. It's relatively easy to create an appealing face of home when a homeowner and architect collaborate on a custom home, but that's not the case where design isn't personalized and cost is everything.

3

This house in New York State by architect Donald Powers is a great example of what can be done to break that mold, and in a way it offers a prototype for suburban houses of the future. This is not your cookie-cutter McMansion; here, quality outshines quantity. What's most appealing about the house is its straightforward imagery and the use of design elements on the exterior that resonate deeply with all of us. The street elevations say it all: A steep main roof with a decorative gable bay, a porch, two-over-two double-hung windows, a breezeway and chimney, shed dormers, and even color are all traditional elements that exude a sense of comfort and familiarity. 1 2

The sheltering pitch of the roof, the porch directed outward to the community 3 , and the warmth implied by the chimney are characteristics that most of us appreciate in any house. Good composition helps tie them together. Here, roof, porch, and chimney are part of a street composition in perfect balance.

Let's look at the front porch in more detail. 4 The porch signals "entry" in a pleasing way, and its low-sloped roof provides just the right balance to the much steeper main gable. Along with a change in color, it also helps to relieve the two-story height of the house and give it a more human scale. Controlling scale by juxtaposing a steep roof and a low-sloped

4

roof is evident elsewhere, such as at the side of the garage 5
and the end of the master bedroom. 6 The breezeway, too,
is a familiar house element; here, it prevents the mass of the
garage from crowding the house, keeping it at arm's length but
not too distant. 7

6

5

7

8

9

10

The design of any suburban house is a challenge. Although the photos of this house make it seem somewhat isolated, the community eventually calls for 150 houses in the neighborhood. The challenge is to create a sense of privacy while still being welcoming. The front porch and breezeway are two inviting gestures, but they're not all that private. So Powers created a more secluded world around the side by enclosing an outdoor garden court, [8] [10] and adding a shared porch off the living room, dining room, and master bedroom. [9]

Fences can sometimes be hard to deal with, especially close up against a house, but this one, with its lattice top, solid bottom, and color to match the first floor of the house, seems well balanced with the rest of the exterior. [11] [12] And in the end, it's a compositional balance, even in the details, that makes this house work so successfully.

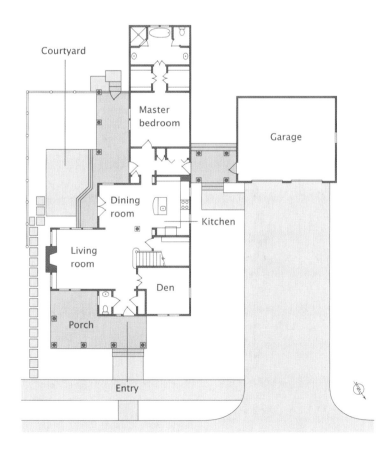

What makes this house such an unusual production house is that it is ornamented with a host of well-designed details, a level of attention that is rarely attained in spec houses built today. The shingled canopy on the entry gable is a good example (see the photo at left). In less talented hands, this element might simply have been two windows set against a steep roof, but here the architect has added a flared roof above the windows with a panel detail in between that combines the two windows into one element. Its softer, sweeping profile also nicely balances the sharper, steeper main roof. The dormer over the garage shows a similar level of attention to detail (see the photo below left).

Windows ganged together in groups, such as those under the shingled canopy at the gable end or at the shed roof dormer, often have a more appealing quality than windows on their own.

Finely detailed wood brackets seem to flow naturally from the main house and add another level of detail that production houses typically don't have (above and bottom of facing page).

White metal-clad window frames with dark contrasting sash provide easy maintenance and a more delicate look.

Windows are an important detail on any house where cost is the major determining factor in what gets built. On this house, the architect has used a relatively maintenance-free aluminum-clad window in two colors. The window frames are white to match the casings, while the sashes are darker, which tends to accentuate the height of the window unit. All of the windows are the same style—two-over-two double-hungs— but the architect has used various sizes to signify the relative importance of the inside spaces. This is a good way to keep an overall visual balance while staying within a budget on a production house.

two-foot cottage

a window shapes the house

Houses can be designed around a lot of things: a good view, an important room, the path of the sun, or what other houses in a historical neighborhood look like. But the design foundation for this Maine island cottage is a simple 2-ft.-square window. My firm used a small vinyl-clad window in a stock size to arrange the look of the cottage, both inside and out. Architects call this kind of basic dimension a *module*, the purpose of which is to build a consistent and pleasing look throughout the house. ① ②

③

4

5

6

This square window shape has an impact on every part of the exterior. On the main southeast elevation, [3] the side of the cottage facing the water, the window is used by itself and in multiples of two, three, and six. Even the larger windows on this wall are 4 ft. by 4 ft., another version of the module. The screen porch, too, is made up of 4-ft.-wide sections of screening.

Move around to the southwest face [4] [5] and you'll see the window's impact again. Although windows don't dominate this side as dramatically as they do on the front of the cottage, they are grouped appropriately for their locations—four units in the kitchen, two in the bathroom, and six for the bedrooms on the second floor. On the northeast side, stacking the basic window floor to eave gives the corner a sense of lightness, literally and figuratively. [6] Placing one window on each side of the chimney gives this elevation a definite facelike quality: The windows are eyes and the tapered chimney could be a nose (see the illustration at right).

two-foot cottage

From a distance, you should be able to get clues about the details that become more dramatic when you get closer. The chimney, for example, is a strong vertical element that's easy to see from afar. [7] Although the stone blends naturally with the surroundings, the chimney is visually powerful, suggesting the importance of the fireplace on the interior. A band of white roof shingles marks a change in roof length from one side of the cottage to the other and tells us where the interior living space ends and the screened porch begins.

As you move closer, other details become more prominent. The rhythm of the board-and-batten siding, for instance, flows naturally from the choice of 2-ft. windows as a basic building block. Battens are arranged on 1-ft. centerlines, exactly half the window dimension [8], bringing further harmony to the exterior. The effect is emphasized by extending the batten strips below the face of the boards, giving the house an interesting fringe-on-the-cuff look. [9] The roof trusses are placed on 4-ft. centerlines, or twice the basic window dimension. They are carried beyond the face of the wall and exposed on the exterior, where they become supporting elements for the roof overhangs and a trellis over the door. [10] In time, the trellis will support a wisteria vine.

8

9

10

Details should express themselves clearly on the outside and the inside. Prefabricated roof trusses are obviously a structural necessity, but because they are left exposed on the interior, as is all the framing, they impart an interior order that bestows a sense of "cottage-ness" (imagine the interior without them and it would have a completely different look). The trusses' rhythm, or order, also is completely consistent with the exterior rhythm of the windows and board-and-batten siding. Inside and outside are literally and visually connected.

Details can have emotional impact or a kind of personality, too. They can seem heavy and serious or impart a sense of whimsy, as the stair rail in this cottage does. There's nothing wrong with a little humor now and then in the design of houses, especially for a cottage. Although the flat-board balusters give the impression of many patterns, especially on the rail overlooking the stair, they are cut from a single pattern and shifted slightly to give that effect.

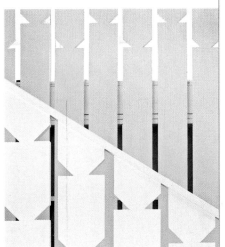

At first glance, the stair balusters seem to be made up of many different patterns but closer examination reveals that it's actually just one pattern slightly offset. Like the rest of the cottage, it's a good example of how visual interest can be achieved through simplicity.

A wall of windows made up of multiples of a basic 2-ft. by 2-ft. module form the most distinctive element of this cottage, inside and out.

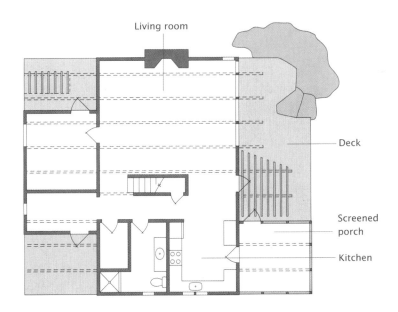

Living room

Deck

Screened porch

Kitchen

rooms in a row

all about the circulation

All houses are made up of a limited palette of materials and spaces. Whether the primary materials are wood, stone, metal, or glass, houses of any given size have mostly the same kinds of rooms—a living room, dining room, kitchen, some bedrooms. So how can one house look so completely different from another? Part of the answer lies in how these spaces are connected, how you move from one room to the next. This is what an architect would call "circulation," and it's the glue that holds a house together. ⑴⑵

6

7

When homeowners list the rooms in their houses, they seldom talk about hallways, stairs, and other means they use to navigate their way around, but no floor plan is successful without these things. Circulation space can be incorporated into the room itself, planned as an adjacent area, or, as is the case with this house, become a strong space all by itself, which is what makes this face of home so intriguing.

That becomes clear even before you're inside this house designed by Good Architecture. As you approach the entry (big, yes, but this one really gets used), you can see down a long hallway that stretches from one end of the house to the other. [3] [4] [5] Although you could also enter the house through either of the garages that flank the entry, you'd still end up at the same hallway, which quickly emerges as a key organizing element of the whole house.

Just inside the front door, something else becomes clear. This is no ordinary hallway because you're still outside the house. Stretched out in front of you is a low, covered, and elegantly detailed walkway with a lawn to one side and rooms to the other. [6] [7] It's now clear that this walkway serves as both outside access to the house and as a connector for the rooms. It wouldn't work in all climates, but here in Virginia, it's perfect.

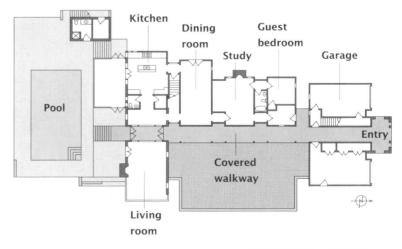

Kitchen
Dining room
Guest bedroom
Study
Garage
Pool
Entry
Covered walkway
Living room

a house of many faces

9

8

The house is actually a series of rooms strung in a row, which is exactly how it appears on the exterior. ☐1 It's almost as if each room is a separate pavilion linked to each other by the circulation space. Whereas most houses have four main elevations, or faces, this one has many.

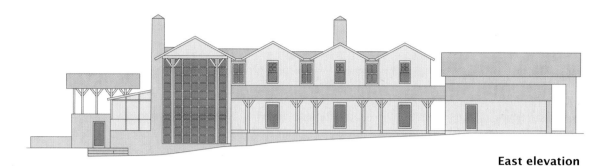

East elevation

This approach has a number of advantages, especially in a warmer climate. It exposes more exterior wall surface for better cross ventilation. It also gives what might otherwise be a visually imposing house a smaller, more human scale by breaking down the mass of the home into more comprehensible parts. 8 9 This is particularly evident on the long east and west sides of the house. Each living space— or living pavilion—on the first floor has a corresponding bedroom above with it own pitched roof.

This is also true on the south side, where the living room and kitchen are separated by the main walkway—the same circulation space that begins at the entry and ends, a few steps down, at the pool. 10 Here again, living and kitchen pavilions are seen as distinct entities on the exterior. Overall, the effect is of a house made up of separate rooms, each with its own dollhouse-like quality, a very different visual strategy than seen in some other houses in this book.

In reality, these spaces aren't detached on the inside. After all, one has to get from one room to the other. The architect has cleverly solved the problem by using glass as the connector, separating each pavilion visually on the outside but allowing spaces to be joined on the inside.

10

mix-and-match materials

Breaking down the volume of a house into smaller pieces is one way of making a large house seem smaller on the outside. Another is to change materials and colors of the walls and roof or add elements and accessory structures, such as porch roofs, brackets, or a pool house. This house uses all of those techniques.

There's a mix of horizontal siding, vertical siding, board-and-batten siding, and even stone on the walls as well as small but finely detailed metal shed roofs over some windows and doors. Color helps to individualize some spaces, as does a change in roof materials: metal in some areas, asphalt shingles in others. All of it helps break down the scale and mass of the exterior into more comprehensible parts. Just imagine this house with walls and roofs of all the same color and material and you can appreciate the effectiveness of the mix-and-match approach.

The wide array of materials used on the exterior (see the photos below) helps break down the pavilions of this house and give them a more human scale.

One of the most appealing results of arranging rooms in a row is getting good views and ventilation from three sides, as you do on this second-floor screen porch off the master bedroom.

A continuous outdoor porch or circulation space connects all the rooms of the house on the first floor. It's the perfect complement for its Virginia setting.

back to the box

a square within a square

Frank Lloyd Wright used to insist that houses should always "break out of the box," but even the greatest of American architects didn't get it right every time. This modest house in Washington State proves that staying within the box can work, too. [1] [2] More restrained than bold, the effect is a bit like listening to a string quartet rather than a brass band.

3

4

The house is really a square within a square. [3] [4] A two-story, 24-ft. square is flanked on two sides by one-story attachments that together make up an overall 36-ft.-square footprint. It's this simple geometry that gives the house its distinctive look. Capping the two-story core is a prominent four-sided hip roof with deep overhangs, the strongest feature of the house. [5] Other elements—a low-roofed master bedroom wing at the northwest corner, a bay in the living room, and even the patios carved out of the volume of the house—all play a secondary visual role. A change in materials from wide horizontal boards on the first floor to shingles on the second floor reinforces the dominance of the central core.

Windows can help you read the inside of the house from the outside. [6] [7] On the first floor, tall windows and a simple shed roof mark a sitting bay in the living room; patio doors and slightly smaller windows indicate the dining room, and even smaller windows mark where the kitchen and baths are likely to be. Each window height is appropriate for its location: big windows for enjoying the view, smaller windows where food is prepared or to ensure privacy. With the exception of the bathrooms, the second-floor walls are almost all window, an equally appropriate way to take advantage of the majestic views. The four panes that form a square for the upper portion of the casement windows are a nice reference to the square plan of the house, and the green paint is a pleasing contrast to the natural finish of the main body of the house.

Utility room

Patio

Entry

Master bedroom

Kitchen

Patio

Living room

Dining room

5

6

7

A simple house should be accompanied by simple details. This doesn't mean they should be uninteresting, just not overwhelming. In this case, the design team of Cascade Joinery has achieved a comfortable balance by using unadorned wood timbers that literally and figuratively support elements of the house. Trellises above the windows and doors in the dining area, for example, consist of brackets that support two layers of timbers that run at right angles to each other. A piece of clear plastic on top lets in the light but keeps out the rain over the door. Besides moderating the sunlight, the trellises add a level of detail that contrasts nicely with the strong, simple forms of the house.

A cutaway corner in the otherwise square plan provides a covered area for relaxing off the living/dining area.

The low one-story roof that encloses the master bedroom continues over a small entry porch, providing the perfect spot for protected storage.

In the bathroom and other rooms of the second floor, the structure and shape of the hip roof are exposed on the ceiling.

The most prominent feature of the house, its hipped roof, is supported at the corners with a finely detailed system of overlapping timbers and brackets, reminiscent of Japanese architecture.

The most prominent feature of this house is its umbrella-like roof, and the most prominent details are the brackets that hold it up. Exposed roof rafters are supported by large horizontal timbers that, in turn, are held up by brackets similar to those on the first floor. This assembly of parts, all in the same material, supports the roof while helping to shade the large second-story windows. But the net effect is more than purely functional; it also imparts to this simple, plain box a kind of elegance in wood similar to the detailing of a Japanese house.

the face of housing

looking out, looking in

All of the houses we've looked at so far have been single-family homes. But what happens to the face of home when a building is more than one house, when it's actually many houses together? The same design principles apply, but because housing projects are larger than any single home, the scale is obviously a lot different. It's also a bigger challenge to give each homeowner his or her own sense of place. One approach is to make each house look unique, but that can be visually confusing and expensive. More typically, the idea is to provide a number of variations within an overall theme, to balance the uniformity of housing with an individual "look" for each homeowner. That's the case here with a 106-unit apartment complex called Tesoro Grove in San Diego, just north of the U.S./Mexico border. [1][2]

3

As with a single-family home, each elevation, or face, of a housing project should respond to its surroundings. Often, however, housing sites can vary dramatically. Here, the site was surrounded by existing housing and busy highways. [3] Studio E Architects cleverly provided a number of faces—some looking out, some looking in—each with its own identity. Along the highway, it's not even clear that these are residences, as all you can see is a series of small windows and a rhythm of buildings broken up by wall recesses. But when you turn down the entrance drive, [4] the project takes on an entirely new face, a new personality, with brighter colors and lively shapes. You are now aware of a number of housing blocks made up of various materials, shapes, and colors that together are much more inviting than what you see from the highway. When you move even closer to the center of the project—here you're mostly on foot—the faces change again. [5] Now, instead of larger blocks, individual units surrounding a grove and community park come into view.

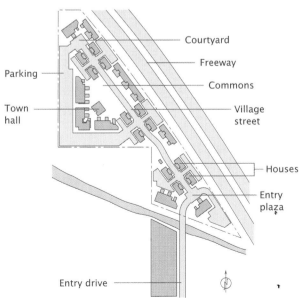

Parking

Town hall

Entry drive

Courtyard

Freeway

Commons

Village street

Houses

Entry plaza

creating a sense of entry

6

7

In a new housing neighborhood, one of the most difficult tasks is to make each house feel like a home among many houses. One way to do that is to individualize the entries to each house. This is not unlike creating a strong exterior sense of entry on a single-family home, one of the major ingredients of any good face of home. This project provides intimate entry paths to some apartments 6, individual stairs to second-level units 7, and small, covered entry porticos. 8 While these exterior architectural elements are repeated throughout the project, their immediate effect is to provide a distinct entry for each homeowner.

8

The selection of materials, windows, and colors on a house is important in achieving a good, balanced exterior. In a housing development, that task is made more difficult by the sheer number of units that must be given an overall sense of unity. Here, the architect has balanced two materials (stucco and smooth cement-board siding), two basic window types (double-hung and casement), and four colors to achieve an exterior read that tells us a lot about each apartment. 9 10 For example, large windows, panelized wood, and the color white are used to differentiate living spaces from accessory spaces. Baths and bedrooms have smaller windows and a stucco exterior and are gray in color. The color yellow is used selectively on some top floors or on a long expanse of units to help break down the mass of some blocks. Picture those areas all in gray, and you can imagine how different the exterior would look.

Downspouts don't have to be straight, especially in a climate where snow and ice aren't a concern. This whimsical downspout adds real zest to a detail that would otherwise be nondescript.

Details are just as important in multifamily housing as they are in a single-family home. One of the major reasons this project feels more like a series of houses than a housing project is that many of its larger components and their details help make each unit seem different. Details can differentiate one apartment from another or enhance an elevation. On the somewhat nondescript highway elevation, the zigzag downspout has a practical function, but it's been turned into a decorative element that's much more appealing than a straight downspout would be, especially when seen from a moving car. This might not work in the colder north, but it's perfect for California.

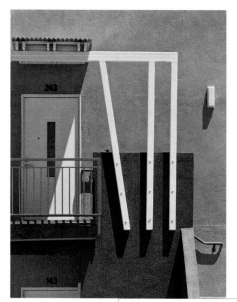

Small details on a large housing project, such as these trellis supports, can give each individual unit its own unique sense of place.

Stairs and bays help
differentiate one unit
from another and give
the housing project
a more human scale.

Other interesting details include the brackets that support the
entry covers and the trellises over the second-floor balconies.
The delicacy of these two details is a nice balance to the larger,
plainer blocks of the apartments. Then there are the bays and
stairs. White projecting bays with wood battened panels and red
stairs balance the mass and scale of the project, defining each
apartment and transforming housing into house.

past and present

natural evolution

Many of the houses in this book are interesting because of contrasts—contrasts between the front and back of the house, for instance, or between different materials or colors. But this house in Waterford, Virginia, designed by Reader & Swartz Architects, is less about contrasts and more about continuity.

3

Building a compatible addition to an early 19th-century house—a cabin, really, of log, chink, and daub construction—isn't easy. Do you build an addition that's simply a clone of the existing house, or do you make the house current with a contemporary addition? Successful renovations blend old and new, bringing a house up to date without neglecting its ancestry. In a poetic way, the architects have done that here.

Take, for example, how different types of siding have been used to emphasize the old and the new parts of the house. There's the board-and-batten vertical siding on the gable ends of the old house and horizontal clapboard siding on the new addition and over the porches at both ends of the house. 1 2 Both siding types are compatible with the old logs, and all of the siding material is essentially traditional in nature. There are no jarring contrasts, and the color white also has a unifying effect. Note, too, the horizontal stripe of trim on the gable end of the old house. 3 It's a small gesture, but it connects the roof edge of the new with the gable of the old house.

4

5

Two entirely different porch elevations give us another link between past and present. The porch facing the old road 4 5 is reminiscent of another era, a day when you wanted to be close enough to the road to greet passersby. Chances are you wouldn't actually sit there today, but its lanternlike glow at night is a wonderful introduction to the house. On the other hand, it's easy to imagine sitting on the new porch around back 6 7 with its more private location and slightly higher elevation. Like the siding, the combination of porches helps to balance past and present uses.

8

The original house was thoughtfully located on a slight rise in the land. From afar, all you would have seen in the 19th century was the house shape, each part clearly expressed with simple, rudimentary forms. [8] Nothing interferes with that vision today. Its uniformly white color and a dark metal roof help to blend the gabled addition with the old house. As you move a bit closer, the distinction between old and new is less blurred. The old house, anchored to the land with its massive chimney and log construction, is playfully balanced with a much lighter, but no less substantial, addition.

A closer look at the same side of the house tells us even more. The wood-framed addition is set back about a foot from the face of the older log house (the resulting corner is a perfect place for the downspout). [9] This plan allows the massive construction of the log house to stand proud of its new wing and the original shapes to remain intact. [10] It's clear that the old house is the spiritual father and the addition its offspring— as it should be. The architects got it right.

9

10

The original construction
is exposed on the interior
but blends seamlessly with
the new work.

A one-of-a-kind bridge with a glass floor not only allows more light into the first floor (from windows above) but also symbolizes the connection between the traditional and more contemporary parts of the house.

Through a slight offset in plan and the use of time-honored materials, the new addition (to the right) is distinctive from but compatible with the original.

In the best houses, details reinforce the connection between inside and outside. The original log with chink and daub was left exposed on the interior, and a new roof was installed over the old to expose the original rafters on the second floor. As it is outside, it's evident on the inside what is old and what is new. But in an effort to introduce more light and a sense of lightness, the architects inserted a glass-floored catwalk crossing over the kitchen and linking the two ends of the house. Once again, the massiveness of the original is balanced with the lightness of the addition.

Let's move back outside for another balancing act of details. Compare the visual weight of the small roof dormer on the addition with the chimney on the old house (see the photo at right). The dormer is a contemporary nod; it almost seems to float on the roof. The chimney is entirely traditional in its look and materials. Despite the obvious differences, they balance each other and help reinforce the overall concept of continuity between past and present.

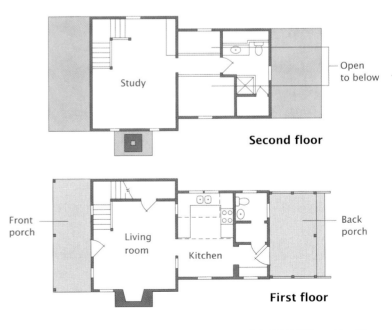

Study

Open to below

Second floor

Front porch

Living room

Kitchen

Back porch

First floor

open to the view

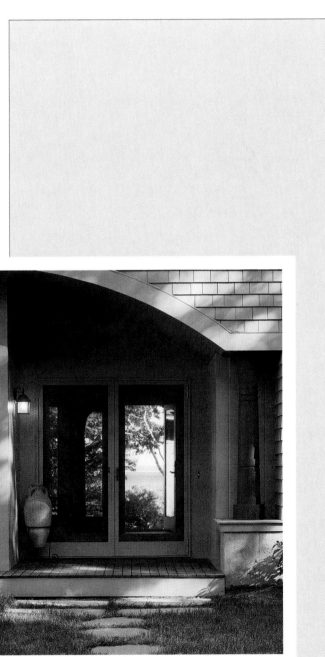

shaped by the site

One of the big problems with a lot of houses built these days is that they are unceremoniously plopped down on the land with no apparent consideration of the site's natural features or how the house will be affected by sun and prevailing weather. Even if you have a good floor plan and an attractive exterior, without careful attention to the relationship between house and site the result just won't work. This house in Woods Hole, Massachusetts, designed by my firm is a good example of the importance of the plan/site relationship and also of how a unique site can actually shape the face of home. ☐1 ☐2

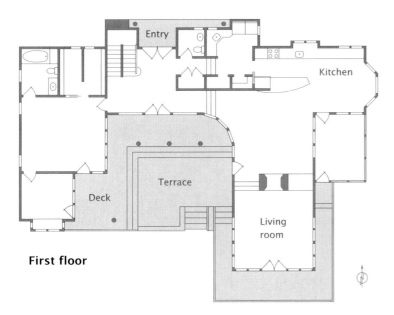

First floor

The house sits on a steep, wooded slope facing the water, property that had been in the family for years. Great care was taken to protect the beech trees lining the extended entrance drive and to preserve the site's woodsy appeal (the house was even stained a light green so it would blend with its surroundings). At the house, the driveway splits into two separate entrances, one at the lower level for everyday family use and the other at the main living level for visitors. This two-level entry is possible because the house is set back into the hillside with the foundation serving as a retaining wall. 3 A long, low-sloping roof reinforces a sense of shelter. At the upper-level entry 4 , a graceful arch serves as a gateway to a courtyard beyond. 5 Standing at the entry, you get the impression you could pass completely through the house from front to back, and you're instantly intrigued to see what lies beyond.

face to the water

6

7

As you pass into the entry hall, it's immediately clear that the main focus of this house is on the outside, not the inside. 6 The dominant feature is an outdoor porch, or more accurately a courtyard, that begins as a covered wood deck and gently steps down to an open, stone terrace that has great views of the water. 7 Every room on the first floor either shares the view or has direct access to the courtyard. 8 Because the house is turned slightly away from the prevailing winds, you can sit in the courtyard and enjoy warm breezes off the water in the summer but be protected from harsh northeast winds in winter. It's also this courtyard that gives the house its distinctive U-shaped look and makes it feel larger than it really is.

Among the most distinctive features of the courtyard are the mahogany columns that support the covered porch roof. [9] [10] The columns have a Middle Eastern flavor (inspired by the owners' travels), and their unique form and contrasting color help define sitting areas along the length of the porch and give the courtyard a better sense of scale. A shorter version of the same column at the front entry aligns perfectly with one of the porch columns, again providing a hint of things to come.

A fireplace that can
be used from both
the living and dining
rooms reinforces the
see-through quality
of the house.

Like the U-shaped plan and window-filled walls, the details in this home encourage an interaction between inside and out. The fireplace is a good example. Rising a story and a half between the dining area and the living room, its see-through design imparts the same sense of visual openness as the rest of the house while making the two adjoining spaces seem larger. Unlike a solid wall, this fireplace encourages interaction among people in the living room, dining room, and even the kitchen.

Outside, railings of stainless-steel cable give this waterfront house a slightly nautical flavor. They are delicate enough not to block the view; a mahogany top rail (softer to the touch than steel) picks up the color and material of the porch columns. Back inside, the hallway stair, with its simple, elegant wood detailing, reinforces the feeling of lightness. Like the courtyard, the chimney, and the railings, the stair stands out as one of the most important visual elements of the house. In fact, when I began the design of this house, I imagined these details even before I thought of the roof and walls. So here the details and plan came first and the exterior evolved naturally.

The elegant stair is part of a two-story hall that serves as a focal point and connector between the interior and the exterior terrace overlooking the water.

The U-shaped plan surrounds a covered porch and open terrace that provide a protected area to enjoy the views year-round.

big and beautiful

getting big right

Big houses get a lot of bad press these days. Part of the reason is that many of them are just plain ugly. There's no other word for it. These sprawling production houses, dubbed "McMansions" by their critics, suffer a variety of shortcomings—uncomfortable proportions, no real relation to the site, and a lack of refined detailing. But it hasn't always been this way: Many of the big houses from the past are quite beautiful. The current problem isn't really about size; it's about bad design. This house by Shope Reno Wharton Associates of Greenwich, Connecticut, is proof that a big house can have a well-proportioned exterior, fit the site, and be full of great details. ☐1 ☐2

3

At 1.8 acres, the lot is not enormous but even this large house fits comfortably. That's because there's a wonderful harmony between house and site, a matching sense of symmetry and formality in both the house design and the landscape design. In reality, the symmetry of the house is not absolute, since a major wing containing the kitchen, family area, outside porch, and garage is off center. ☐3 So is the pool. In a truly symmetrical house, you'd expect wings of equal size on each side of the house. Truth is, the site was too small for that arrangement, but it doesn't feel as if there's a wing missing. Because all the major elements of house, pool, and site are aligned in a clear order, or what architects call "on axis," the result is an overall sense of composure and balance.

This sense of symmetry and formality is what holds the house and site together visually, but if you look closely you'll find that certain parts of the house have a quite different feel. At the kitchen, family room, and garage wing on the north side, the house drops some of its formality and presents a different but equally appealing face. ☐4 ☐5 This is the everyday entry side, and it has a more informal air and an asymmetry emphasized by the sparseness of white detailing in wood and a lower roof height. It's as if the house has public and private faces, both different but both appropriate.

4

5

Site Plan

Pergola

Pool

Formal garden

Informal entry

Main house

Formal entry

Street

a sense of order

Most people find the strong sense of order and symmetry in this house inherently appealing because it evokes a feeling of tranquility. Instead of darting from one feature to another, your eyes tend to focus on the overall composition. But what contributes to such order? Windows and doors on each floor are mostly the same size and are equally placed to the right and left of the center of the house, as are the stone chimneys on the roof. [6] The windows and doors seem to have just the right amount of white wood to offset the visual weight of the stone. Certainly this house could have been all stone, but the delicately detailed wood throughout helps to impart a sense of balance. The repetition of columns, keystones above doors and windows, and even the equal-sided hip roof on the main body of the house reinforce the sense of order and balance. [7]

The most prominent features of the house are the slightly projecting entry bays on both front and back. Positioned dead center on the main body of the house, each has it own gable or pedimented roof over a three-part window with an arched section in the middle. Often referred to as a Palladian window, this central feature acts as a visual anchor for other parts of the house around it. Look again, though, at both the front and the back and you'll see that there's a slight difference between the two entry bays. The formal entry court side has a projecting porch and formal door with sidelights, while the other side of the house has no porch roof at all but large, uncovered French doors facing a sunny formal garden. [8] Those differences are evident inside, too. On the formal side of the house, there's a two-story entry hall [9], whereas on the garden side, there's a quiet sitting room looking out over the garden. So even while a strong, formal order is the most apparent organizing feature of the house, subtle variations respond to specific needs. It's the balance of these two characteristics that makes this face of house so satisfying.

6

7

8

9

A rounded bay fits nicely into a south-facing inside corner and recalls the rounded shapes found on details elsewhere on the house, such as the Palladian windows and the interior archways.

A substantial house requires substantial details. Here, three columns—not just one—at an outside porch corner, provide enough visual weight to be consistent with the rest of the house.

The consistency of fine detailing, inside and out, helps to give this big house its sense of order and balance. It's a quality that's conspicuously absent on so many large production houses built today. From a distance across the lawn and right into the interior, dormers, brackets, and columns work together to reinforce the overall composition. Like the Palladian window, an all-wood, rounded sitting bay tucked into the southeast corner of the low wing has a cabinetlike quality. It provides an accentuated pivot point as the house turns the corner, and its finely detailed dollhouse quality provides an intimacy that is sorely lacking in most big houses.

The elaborate white wood fascia and soffit roof trim are balanced by similar wood detailing on the interior. The wood softens the edges between materials and, particularly on this house exterior, keeps the stone from being too overwhelming. Round wood columns used on the porch are matched in the entry hall. Even the keystones over the exterior doors and windows are repeated on the interior archways. On any good face of home, details should never be arbitrary but rather reinforce the house. That's just what they do on this beautiful big house.

Some house details are used on both the interior and exterior. On the exterior, a stone keystone is used to designate a window or door opening; on the interior, the same keystone in wood is used over arched passageways.

house of many faces

wing division

Most houses have four faces—a front, a back, and two sides—and one dominant color. But this tried-and-true approach to design can sometimes produce massive, blocky buildings that seem out of scale with the people who live in them. One way to break up the exterior visually and make the house less imposing is to add overhangs, wings, and bays. But a more radical approach is to divide the house into a number of separate wings or buildings, as Fernau & Hartman Architects has done with this house in Sonoma County, California. [1][2] By my count, there are 14 different faces on this house, resulting in a house with a smaller, friendlier scale. Vibrant colors enhance the effect.

4

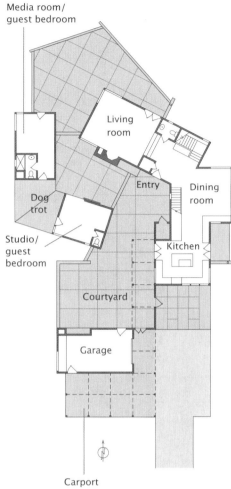

Media room/
guest bedroom

Living
room

Entry

Dining
room

Dog
trot

Studio/
guest
bedroom

Kitchen

Courtyard

Garage

Carport

Like any well-designed house, this one takes advantage of its site. It's built on the ridge of a hill, nestled near a large pine tree 3 , with its various wings and outbuildings wrapping around a flat plateau. From afar, the variety of shapes and colors might lead you to think this is more than a single house. 4 It's not, of course, and as you approach you realize that shape, color, and even exterior materials are used to suggest that different parts of the house have different functions. Living, sleeping, and study spaces are contained in one building of stucco and wood, colored in yellow and red. 5 Spaces for guests, studios, and garage are in three separate wood buildings stained blue-green. Mixing colors and materials this way is a California building tradition, and it helps to show the plan on the outside, perhaps more dramatically here than in any other house in this book.

5

blocks of color

6

Designing the house as several buildings instead of one means there are more walls with windows and, therefore, better views and more light on the inside. It also means the buildings can be placed so they form a courtyard that offers protection from the weather on this exposed site. [6] Since all the rooms have access to this outdoor living space, it serves a practical purpose. But it's also visual anchor for the site, what the architect calls "a modest, rural Acropolis."

You might imagine that all these shapes and faces of different colors would lead to mass confusion, but they don't because each part is clearly defined. Look, for example, at the master bedroom and study wing on the second floor, colored in red. [7] It's not centered over the first-floor living room but seems almost to slice through the main body of the building. Its smaller scale is played off against the long, low-sloping roofs of the two adjacent bedroom wings, which are painted yellow. Here, shapes and colors on the exterior say something special about the interior: This is the master bedroom.

7

What makes this second-floor bedroom even more interesting is the way it projects into the interior just over the entry area, carrying the exterior material and color with it. 8 This surprising intrusion of the clapboard inside enlivens the two-story entry space next to the stairs and balances nicely with the more finely detailed wood paneling on the wall of the entry and the more serene living space beyond. 9

A simple courtyard, bounded by the various buildings that make up the house, serves as a visual and practical focal point for the entire compound. Pergolas, benches, and a fountain add another level of comfort.

The introduction of metal sunscreens over some of the windows not only has the practical effect of shielding harsh afternoon sunlight but also adds a somewhat whimsical eyebrow/eyelash quality to the exterior.

Other details have the same effect, offering practical advantages as well as just the right visual touch in the overall scheme of things. Take the metal screens that are cabled off the stucco walls over the high, south-facing windows. They temper direct sunlight almost like eyelashes or eyebrows over an eye, but the screens and the shadows they cast also add another layer of texture to the house. A small concrete fountain in the courtyard next to a bench introduces a new material to the exterior mix, and the sound of water helps make the courtyard a place for quiet reflection as well as outdoor activity (see the photo below).

Sound is one of the least used architectural effects. Here, a simple concrete fountain adds a subtle rhythmic whisper to the atmosphere of the courtyard.

A variety of shapes, materials, and colors gives this house its interesting, almost enigmatic personality, and the supporting details underscore the effect. Take, for example, the pergola that softens the blank garage wall and leads across the courtyard from the garage to the kitchen entry. Made from wood left natural, the pergola lends balance to the more solid feel of other parts of the house exterior and their more vibrant colors. Along with the wood benches in the courtyard, this detail helps to unify the various parts of the house into a community of buildings (see the photos on the facing page).

split decision

making the past contemporary

At first glance, this house on Block Island looks as though it might be two older homes—one big, one small—that were built close together and connected at some time with a porch. [1] But looks can be deceiving. What appear to be two traditional houses are really wings of the same house, and the connector between them is the true core of the home. [2]

The inspiration for this contemporary house, designed by Estes/Twombly Architects, comes from the traditional houses of fishermen and farmers on this island off the coast of Rhode Island. Early houses on the island were often austere, one room deep and two stories high with steep, gabled roofs. The compact hall-and-parlor plan was adequate for the 19th century, but it clearly doesn't suit today's lifestyles.

Overall, the visual impression on the outside is of a house from the past. [3] [4] [5] Each house, or wing, contains bedrooms. On the first floor, the living and dining spaces and the kitchen are joined under a low-sloped, cathedral-ceiling connector in an open floor plan. The connector is cleverly packed with an entry hall, study, master bath, and porches—both open and screened—on the front and back. The decision to split the house offers other amenities too, such as more cross ventilation and better views, especially from the second floor. [6] And, of course, it is the split design that gives the house its novel face of home and places it squarely in our time.

3

4

First floor

Kitchen

Dining room

Living room

Master bedroom

Study

Entry

Outdoor shower

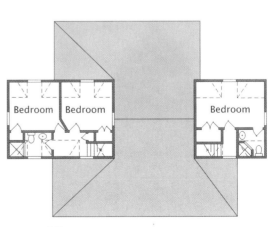

Second floor

Bedroom

Bedroom

Bedroom

the house in context

8

7

From a distance, the house looks a lot like all of the others around it: a solid box with weathered shingles and sparsely painted white trim. 7 It is only when you move in closer that it's apparent the house is actually split in two, and even then its parts and pieces have a traditional feel. 8 You also get the sense that there's nothing haphazard about how the pieces have been positioned. Each contributes to a well-composed whole.

The low-sloped connector has a metal roof, which distinguishes it from the steeper roofs of the two wings, and the entry-porch side of the house is painted yellow to distinguish it from the gray shingles on the rest of the house. **9** Taken together, roof and color mark the connector as a unique feature and show unmistakably where to enter the house. Once on the entry porch, you can see that the house is unlike any around it in another way: It's open from front to back. **10** The entry hall opens to a living area that, in turn, opens to a covered deck and screened porch beyond. The exposed roof framing carries from inside to outside to reinforce this connection.

9

10

subtle details

Simple shapes, windows, and materials are traditional Block Island themes, used here in intriguing ways that place this house in both past and present.

A flat board turned ninety degrees and given a flared edge becomes an unusual but simple newel post.

The detailing on this house is relatively spare, but a number of unobtrusive design decisions hold together well and contribute to the overall visual effect. Take the outdoor shower, for example. Just off to the right of the entry porch and connected by a door to the master bath, the shower is hidden from view by an extension of the yellow siding. Gaps between the siding (for ventilation) are the only hint that the shower is there (see the center photo at left).

The selection and placement of windows offer another opportunity for subtle detailing. Oversized, two-over-two double-hung windows and doors with transoms are used at the center of the house, where light and transparency are most important. Smaller, more standard-sized double-hung windows occupy less prominent locations (bedrooms, kitchen, and study), and even smaller two-over-two awning windows are used at the bathrooms and powder rooms, where privacy is more important than a view. Each window is topped with a tiny cap (known as an *entablature*) with just enough overhang to shed water. On the gable-end wall with the bulkhead doors to the cellar, (see the top photo at left), the architect could have simply aligned the two windows directly over each other (as on the gable at the opposite end of the house. That would have been the typical approach. But by aligning the top window with the centerline of the gable and the bottom window with the centerline of the cellar doors, the architect manages to tie the rather mundane, prefabricated bulkhead to that elevation.

The newel posts at the bottom of the stairs are another example of how one small detail can animate the whole. The stair parts are off the shelf, available from any local lumberyard, but by turning the newels—actually just flat boards—perpendicular to the balusters and flaring them, the architect has given the stair a life and character it wouldn't otherwise have. In a way, that uncommon decision is consistent with many of the other uncommon decisions in this house outside and in.

Featured Architects

Salmela Architects
852 Grandview Avenue
Duluth, MN 55812
(218) 724-7517

northern light (p. 36)

Van Dam Architecture and Design
66 West Street
Portland, ME 04102
(207) 775-0443
www.vandamdesign.com

a symphony of roofs (p. 44)

The Miller Hull Partnership
Polson Building
71 Columbia Sixth Floor
Seattle, WA 98104
(206) 682-6837
www.millerhull.com

straight-faced (p. 52)

Jeremiah Eck Architects
560 Harrison Avenue, Suite 403
Boston, MA 02118
(617) 367-9696
www.jearch.com

change of face (p. 60)

Steven Ehrlich Architects
10865 Washington Boulevard
Culver City, CA 90232
(310) 838-9700
www.s-ehrlich.com

light and solid (p. 70)

Robert Gurney Architects
113 South Patrick Street
Alexandria, VA 22314
(703) 739-3843
www.robertgurneyarchitect.com

two-faced neighbor (p. 78)

Jeremiah Eck Architects
560 Harrison Avenue, Suite 403
Boston, MA 02118
(617) 367-9696
www.jearch.com

the shoebox challenge (p. 86)

Koning Eizenberg Architecture
1454 25th Street
Santa Monica, CA 90404
(310) 828-6131
www.kearch.com

house in garden (p. 94)

Lester Walker
59 Mill Hill Road
Woodstock, NY 12498

built over time (p. 102)

The Office of Peter Rose
One Kendall Square, Building 1700
Cambridge, MA 02139
(617) 494-0202
www.opr1700.com

breaking symmetry (p. 110)

Burr and McCallum Architects
PO Box 345
720 Main Street
Williamstown, MA 01267
(413) 458-2121
www.burrandmccallum.com

craftsman companion (p. 118)

Elliot Elliot Norelius Architecture
86 Main Street, PO Box 318
Blue Hill, ME 04614
(207) 374-2566
www.elliottelliottnorelius.com

see-through house (p. 126)

Donald Powers Architects
146 Clifford Street
Providence, RI 02903
(401) 272-4724
www.donaldpowersarchitects.com

production perfect (p. 134)

Jeremiah Eck Architects
560 Harrison Avenue, Suite 403
Boston, MA 02118
(617) 367-9696
www.jearch.com

two-foot cottage (p. 142)

GOOD/Architecture
132 West Street
Annapolis, MD 21401
(401) 268-7414
www.goodarchitecture.com

rooms in a row (p. 150)

The Cascade Joinery
1401 Sixth Street
Bellingham, WA 98225-7365
(360) 527-0199 (310) 838-9700
www.cascadejoinery.com

back to the box (p. 158)

Studio E Architects
2411 Second Avenue
San Diego, CA 92101
(619) 235-9262
www.studioearchitects.com

the face of housing (p. 164)

Reader & Swartz Architects
2 North Cameron Street
Winchester, VA 22601
(540) 665-0212
www.readerswartz.com

past and present (p. 174)

Jeremiah Eck Architects
560 Harrison Avenue, Suite 403
Boston, MA 02118
(617) 367-9696
www.jearch.com

open to the view (p. 182)

Shope Reno Wharton Associates
18 West Putnam Avenuw
Greenwich, CT 06830
(203) 869-7250
www.shoperenowharton.com

big and beautiful (p. 190)

Fernau & Hartman Architects
2512 Ninth Street, Number 2
Berkeley, CA 94710
(510) 848-4480
www.fernauhartman.com

house of many faces (p. 198)

Estes/Twombly Architects
79 Thames Street
Newport, RI 02840
(401) 846-3336
www.estestwombly.com

split decision (p. 206)